SUDDENLY
IV

Prose Poetry and Sudden Fiction

**Edited by
Jackie Pelham**

Stone River Press
A Page One Publications Imprint
Houston, Texas

SUDDENLY
IV

Prose Poetry and Sudden Fiction

Edited by Jackie Pelham

© 2001

Individual story copyright by authors and used with permission
Book design and typesetting by Jackie Pelham
Cover Design by Jesse Johnson
Introduction by John Gorman

The following have or will appear in other publications: ".38 Grief" is
an excerpt from "Emissary," a work in progress; "The Pigeons" in
Millennium Science Fiction and Fantasy;

Library of Congress Catalog Card Number: 2001117650

Printed in the United States of America

Published by

Stone River Press
A Page One Publications Imprint
281-440-6701

ISBN 0-9627844-7-8

To Christopher Woods
because . . . .

Table of Contents

ix

Foreword

Congratulations to the eighty-nine authors who have been selected to participate in *Suddenly IV*. As was true last year, we have put the authors in alphabetical order with their story and or poem grouped together. Sometimes this makes it difficult to distinguish poetry from fiction, but that's half the fun. This issue should be called the Houston Connection as many submissions were from that area, but we yearn for contributors from all over Texas.

John Gorman, that wonderful orator, poet and teacher agreed to write the introduction. He teaches literature and creative writing at the University of Houston at Clear Lake, and is among the most respected and sought after speakers for local functions. Among his publications are *Perry Como Sings* and *Public Places,* both published by Mac*Kinations Press. The UH-CL recently printed *The Oxford of the Floodplain* as part of its 20th Anniversary celebration. John not only writes poetry but is also published in the fiction genre. Always willing to lend his expertise and jovial attitude, he is a great asset to the writing community. We thank him for his contribution to *Suddenly IV*.

When most of the submissions were from authors I knew, it was still difficult selecting the pieces, because it hurts to send a rejection almost as much as to receive one. Believe me, I've been on the rejected end more times than I like to admit. With over four hundred entries, and since book space is limited, it was necessary to return many good stories and poems. Also, we might have selected a similar piece. If you didn't get in this time, try again. Texas writers are the reason the anthology exists.

As always, thanks to Guida Jackson and William Laufer for their friendship and to Patsy Burk, the best little ol' proofreader around.

And thanks to the contributors for their wonderful stories and poems. We hope in some small way *Suddenly* is a stepping stone for the careers of new writers. For those authors already established, thanks for letting us showcase your work.

—*Jackie Pelham*
April, 2001

Introduction

It's a striking experience, you'll discover if you wish, to read *Suddenly IV* straight through. And it's an honor to be asked to introduce this array of sizzling jolts and decisive landings. But it turns out that a more beautiful intro than I was likely to contrive was already there in code. As I read, I jotted memorable phrases. Soon they began making a poem. Seven artists in, I had The Message. In the *Suddenly* spirit, let it set itself paragraphically:

> *That Certain Soul, The Marrow of Speech*
> Battered humanity walked in rags, without his
> instrument he was nothing. Born to analyze, to
> peel away the skin's every emotion, missing
> nothing, you understand what you want to.

This could have gone on—I assure you, Nancy, Irene, Sharon, all ye who have not been caught without your instruments amid the batterings of life. Understanding probably does come in bolts, Joycean epiphanies, a further justification of the praise Christopher Woods heaped on Jackie Pelham and her distinguished company in his note at the head of *Suddenly III*. Over the years, and may there be many, these gatherings will be an index of the Texan and Human (for indeed can those categories *always* be at odds?) Spirit. And a sequential reading of the Contributors' Notes—I did that too, I'm thorough—shows us once again that Texas is both a province and the world, gathering and sending forth and regathering people and ideas from everywhere.

The she's and he's of *Suddenly IV* give us Vaporub and a Texas Star quilt in a room facing a pecan mott. They give us lighted temples "on the edge of cement waters." Reality plain and *sur*. What a good idea *Suddenly* was and how productively, by dint of much love and labor, it has brought forth its works.

xi

Congratulations to all involved.

I'll conclude, if I may, with a second Found Poem. *And* there's a prize. Truly this is the Intro-with-Everything. Let me know where the elements of the three-liner below come from and win a FREE walking tour of the Bayou Building at the University of Houston-Clear Lake!

The nail of poetry
Irrational lifeboat
Invisible hope.

—John Gorman
June 2001

Poems and Stories

Aunt Dot

Married to my Uncle Hervè; not a blood relative, never friends, but like a Christmas pudding, hastily assembled, we mixed together for holidays, family gatherings. Twenty years between us crossed out closeness. You kept the simmer of your life quiet the way a tight fitting lid covers a pot, leaving only indistinct vapors to rise—about the child you tried to adopt that didn't work out, your money worries, Uncle Hervè's move to my grandparents' house. You never divulged your thoughts. This summer's trip to Little Compton I saw your family's farm; sienna-soft photos of you with a group of teens sitting on the beach, sailing. I learned your mother, a foundling brought over from England, taken up by a nice family, was thrust into an orphanage when the woman died,

(Men could not raise Young Girls alone.) Like a woman in a spell who's afraid to open her mouth for fear strange creatures will emerge, you never told me what you thought, let me know who you were. You had only me to look after you—hospital, nursing floor, assisted living, hospital, funeral. That last hospital day, you spoke to me, *If* this is death, let's get on with it, then slept away your substance. Scientists have figured out what percentages of water, minerals, bone we own; how much the brain weighs. But when we die, that certain soul, the marrow of speech leaves and we can only list what's left.

> Two hearing aids
> Pair of glasses
> Bathrobe
> Tennis shoes

V.T. ABERCROMBIE

Like it or Not

For Stephen Dobyns

These are the days of winter. Morning chill hardens the lining of lungs as each cold breath forces small-line fractures the way a glass carafe breaks, while sodden leaves pretend to be soles on the woman's slippers making the retrieval of the morning paper an uncertain event. The dog greets the woman on the doorstep having better sense than to go out in the face of its own arthritic legs, says, Let's go to Randall's and buy lots of junk food. Let's turn up the heat and lie on soft pillows. This is how dogs deal with unpleasant situations. But in the smell of the kitchen, the woman is stuck with Calphalon skillets and slick plastic spoons, with phantom diapers drying next to shrinking blue jeans, memories shifting and changing the way wine's taste changes with heat. The dog says, Let's go out and give Paco a thrill, I feel the menses coming on. Let's lie inside in the sun feeling sexy. Above the stove, the woman notices the vent filter loaded with grease. Like in a calendar, months layered like wallpaper, breakfasts, lunch and dinners. She thinks of the air escaping, pulled from the house accompanied smells, pot roast, frying chicken, burned rolls, coffee. She wonders where it all went. Is that air hovering, still, over the flat roof of her house, mixing with today's pollutants, or is it crystallized like pebbles on the roof keeping the weather at bay? The dog says, Look, my eyes are gone bad, white with cataracts and I can't hear a damn thing. Are you stomping around doing nothing? Let's have one of those beef jerky chewys at least. But the woman has a vision. Fill the sink with hot soapy suds, get out the Ajax and scrub brush, take down the metal filter, get it really clean, shiny bright, all the holes unplugged, until it's back in place and the exhaust fan hums easily, expels all the air, pulling first from the kitchen, then all the other rooms, like taffy, stretching thinner and thinner, graceful in its leaving. The dog says, For pity's sake, I'm in the bedroom minding my own business while you're messing around in there. It's getting hard to breathe in here. Knock it off. The woman stands in the kitchen admiring the last of the wisps snaking toward the fan. She turns it off, gets out a can of dog food, a chicken to microwave for dinner, looks out the window toward what she now considers her air, reflected off a cloud the way light from street lamps puddles on rainy streets, the way an electric burner on high fades slowly when you turn it off.

KAYE VOIGT ABIKHALED

Mattress Companion

These days I sleep with a fat New Yorker beside me—at my age one takes what one can get. There are better ones I could choose, more pliable, accommodating, of better quality, but this one has a yellow attraction all his own: heavy rustling shakes the mattress at late night, a careless spine that heaves its weight onto my chest and startles me awake when dozing. It matters little that my resting space is usurped for I have found I can lay my head on, cradle, pat and stroke, inhale his breathing fire, accept desire of grasping attention, then letting go and I rock with a flow and motion full-bodied, monstrous, going back in time more years than I am willing to acknowledge: well experienced, hugely rounded, naturally corpulent, all virtues I can trust, offerings of mutual benefit. To be fair, I must thank the parents who created such a sage, mighty mass who shares my nights: Regards and deep affection to the editors of *The New Yorker Book of Poems* with all its eight-hundred-and-thirty-five pages.

KAYE VOIGT ABIKHALED

1945

Allied fighting forces came upon cities in ruin. Battered humanity walked in rags, in leftover men's clothing, hugging soiled pillows, lugging fraying curtain pieces tied in bundles, women and children hiding hair-loss under tightly knotted scarves, hanging on to teeth too loose to chew, walking a hulking gait in fearful trepidation. A society of females and underage children without men.

American fighting troops shocked at the sight, hid tears of compassion behind hunched shoulders under helmets pulled low over wet lashes, intently staring at maps and military orders, blaming an icy wind for falling tears, doing a job, not judging.

British forces advancing eastward in their northern sector of Europe took stock, appropriated, confiscated anything of value, incarcerating professionals for later evaluation, eagerly pursuing their contest with American troops in moving eastward to meet up with their Russian allies.

Russians came crushing west in hordes. A louse infested flea-bitten humanity, theirs was the campaign of retribution, avenging the lives of their lost. They tore chandeliers from ceilings, ripped flowered porcelain toilets from pipes and took them to their tundra huts, expecting light and working sewerage. They confiscated wrist watches, strapping them to both arms up to their elbows, listening mesmerized to the tiny tick-tick, and with a gesture of regret, exchanged them for others when mechanisms unwound. *Uhri kaput.* With fiendish passion they pried from hiding places struggling females, and raped and raped, spreading syphilis and pregnancy to horrified women gone insane, who climbed ruins of multi-story buildings, hanging for days onto exposed pipes and window frames, screaming in voices no longer human, howling their accusations against the world, against God, until finally exculpating they flung themselves to their deaths writing the final chapter in a cruel war of a thousand year Reich that lasted barely twelve.

ANN K. ANDERSON

Jean Luc's Awakening

Jean Luc twitched, mumbling as the bed covers gathered in knots around his sweating body.

He wanted out of the dream that came often these nights, but it continued on its relentless course.

He stood on a podium in front of a vast orchestra. Fifty-seven pairs of musicians' eyes followed his every movement. He tried to breathe but his chest felt solid with no room for air.

What was happening? He was a violinist. Without his instrument he was nothing. He looked left and right . . . it was no where in sight.

A music stand containing a score he could scarcely see separated him from the orchestra. He hoped the music was something he could conduct easily, since it seemed that was what was expected of him.

Behind him the audience sat hushed.

How long had he been standing here?

He leaned forward and squinted at the score. Richard Strauss's Suite from *Der Rosenkavalier.* At least he knew the piece intimately. Had played it often. But why was he here instead of sitting in the first chair violinist's position?

Sweat rolled down his cheek, setting up an involuntary tic. His fellow violinists were beginning to look nervous. Several dropped their arms, lowering their bows. He heard coughs and whispers from the audience.

He had no idea how to begin.

Jean Luc rolled over in bed, fighting with his pillow. This was a dream. It was time for it to stop. It had never gone this far before. The sheer terror of the situation had always awakened him. But tonight the dream rolled on, relentless in its determination to shatter his will.

He pushed himself erect on the podium. Reached forward to pick up the baton he saw mocking him from the music stand. He knew music. He could do this.

And then it came to him. When he played the violin, he first created the sound he wanted to produce in his head. He shaped and molded it, refining, blending tones, reaching for perfection. Only then would he allow the sound to escape from his violin.

Recently he'd discovered he had the ability to teach that technique to other violinists. But could he influence more than fifty musicians to create beautiful sounds in their minds and then let those perfect tones escape from their instruments? It was one thing to mold the sound of one violin, but to mold the magnificence of a full orchestra . . . how could one man ever attain such heights?

Behind him, the audience fidgeted. Before him, the orchestra waited, alert, wary.

He had no choice. He had to try.

Jean Luc glanced at the score once more. Imagined his violin part, then filled in the other instruments. After a few bars, he realized everyone was playing, all the harmonies were there. His hands and arms were moving, pumping, expanding the sound, contracting it, allowing it to surge and beat and grow around him.

Individual instruments lost their definition and became expressions of emotion. Jean Luc became part of the musical story, feeling Sophie and Octavian's passions, experiencing their pain. Strauss was all about emotion. Emotion and pomp and grandeur. Jean Luc allowed the impassioned music to inflame him, to flow through his head and hands and body into the orchestra, filling him until the piece was over.

Jean Luc lowered his arms.

Hair rose on the back of his neck as the silence deepened.

And then the roar. The audience stood as one, a great cheer bursting from their throats. Jean Luc knew he had touched them. Allowed them to join in his emotional journey.

21

He had opened himself and not been found wanting.

He awoke smiling. Intermezzo, his cat, meowed softly and rubbed against him. With Intermezzo came reality.

He was not the person he'd just dreamed himself to be. Even as a child he'd never learned to display emotions. He rolled over and tried to find the oblivion of sleep. Before it came, he began to know the real meaning of need.

GEORGE AYRES

Blood on the Wall

When I look out the window all I can see is her reflection. It fills the glass like a disfigured Greek statue. Striking and serious and it won't go away. She was born to analyze and peel away the skins of every emotion, every response, every facial expression. And after that, the pain of the crying always comes until there's soreness about the eyes and your head hurts. There's no way around that part. I want her to stop but she won't. I'm not man enough to stop her. I'm not man enough to admit she's right. The words are heavy as concrete on my skull and the shimmering neon outside in the darkness makes me sick to my stomach. Cigarettes burn in the ashtray down to nothing but we don't care. She won't be quiet about my smallness as a person, my fear to give her one inkling of the truth. I could jump from here and not feel it. I think for a second that's what I'll do, but the thought washes away from me, drifts away like the tide, changes everything in its path from here on out. Every part of me is a product of erosion. I, for one, can see it on my face and feel it in my bones. Right down to the marrow. I think she'll get violent soon. She's prone to that and I've got the scars to prove it. I want to rip my brain out and pin it to the wall. Right next to the ugly Uzilevsky print–customary artwork for rooms at this price range. Figure out where I went wrong in the jumbled mess that looks like a poorly diagrammed sentence. There I'd be, finally the analyzer, blood dripping down the wall, trying to locate the misfire, the gap in the wiring, the burnt fuse. Trying to discover where in my history I thought it was okay to be the bastard I turned into. I can't face her. I can't admit anything now and still she rants. I can't even lie anymore. Our togetherness is fiery and turbulent, pushing each other as far

23

as we can, as close as we can to the thin ice over water. Then we wait and watch. Meet in one of these rooms and see which one will put their foot out and step on the watery glass. Which one will get chilled to the bone. Primal, fiercely connected at the soul, we fight like caged animals for a piece of each other, then take turns sewing our skins back on while we brush back our bangs from the tears. It may be best to end it but we won't let that happen. It would take away the oxygen and if a thing has no breath . . . well. . . .

Scarlet darkness shadows the room now and there's something Christ-like about the color of it, some complex late night sacrament, but I'm not ready to figure it out. She won't be quiet. She's right about everything. I can't take much more. My head is pounding. Lord knows I deserve the beating I'm taking.

WENDY BARKER

Macramé

I never got into it. Too many knots. Rope or string, mostly white, or that pale yellowy color, twisted in on itself, maybe a few beads. All that work just to hold a houseplant off the floor. I learned to weave. Different yarns. Crinkly silk like hair from an unraveled braid. Silver. A fat wool, furry, the shade of lichen under a pine. And blue, a deep teal, turquoise, the way you remember an inland high sky in winter. Purple, fuchsia, orange—sunsets. Dawn. Sometimes I thought of the students I liked while I worked. Frances, her low voice, her cello. Jennifer's little giggles. James, his wide smile, Afro. Andrew, always trying to get me to read *Dune*. The warp strands sturdy, brown. Backstrap loom tied to the window latch. I pushed the weft threads down, a soft thud. Over and under. One color showing more now, another the next time. I gathered eucalyptus bells that fell under the tall trees in the hills. Clean smelling, a good medicine. I liked working the dark seeds into the pattern. I wanted to make something big, fill a space, soften a wall.

WENDY BARKER

Gimme Five

Julie was always high-fiving somebody. The principal, the coaches, the head counselor, even Willie Jones when he told her he hadn't missed one class in the last six weeks, no blue slip sent home to his mother this time. Anybody male, she held out her palm, her bright red nails facing the floor, and said "gimme five," her San Francisco private girls school speech dropping east, down, and south by half a dozen states. She even did the lean forward, the dip down from the hips with the back straight and almost horizontal to the ground, one knee lifting up toward the chin, and finally, the laugh. I could never get it right. But you didn't see the other women teachers doing it, especially not any of the black women. And you never saw them in skirts as short as Julie's. True, the girls' track coach Louise walked around in her little gym shorts all the time, but you never saw the Latin teacher Ardis Baine or Roberta Gibson, with her groomed little Afro, in a skirt much above their knees. Julie was almost one of the guys—talked football, basketball, passes, tight ends, overtime with all of them. Only a few people knew about her mother, so bad an alcoholic she couldn't even look up to focus on whoever came through the door, let alone put an arm around her daughter's shoulder. Been that way off and on for years. And her father—I met him once at their clothing store. He gave me a discount. But I heard him complaining to Julie, he wished his daughter could help him out sometimes on the floor. He was sure she had some spare time once in a while, she didn't have to teach on weekends did she, couldn't she give him a five-hour stretch once a month or so?

WILLIAM McCARGO BARNES

A Man Called Rimfire

My unwavering gaze slowly scans every object on the dusty street; missing nothing. Concentrated attention to detail keeps me alive for more years than I care to admit.

From my position on the bench in front of the only saloon in town, I peer from beneath my black, broad-brimmed hat and watch dust devils traverse the road that extends north across the featureless prairie toward the railroad. I turn toward the south and see the mountains of Mexico, distorting the horizon into a saw-toothed edge.

My gun hand rests lightly on my thigh, made hard and lean by many years in the saddle.

I watch the tall stranger walking slowly toward me with the early-morning sun behind him, forcing me to squint against the glare. There is something familiar about that slow, measured gait.

Smart, I think. Just the direction I would approach from. This stranger bears cautious observation.

Careful not to make any sudden moves, I edge over to the center of my bench, not taking any chances with this newcomer. Though he appears to be unarmed, he has the look of a shooter.

Lotta places a man can hide a Derringer, I remind myself.

The stranger stands an erect six feet. Long, unruly hair hangs low enough to touch his collar.

He wears his gray, wide-brimmed Stetson pulled low over his eyes, cavalry-style. I count three bullet holes in it.

Matching the stubble on his chin, bunches of white hair sprout from each nostril like prickly pear growing from twin prairie-dog holes.

His worn shirttail hangs out of dusty and partially buttoned pants. What appears to be a dried bloodstain covers one thigh. He looks as if he's been to Hell and back.

My dun stands hitched at the rail, tail swishing in annoyance at the flies.

"Your horse?" he asks.

"He ain't for sale," I say.

"Didn't ask if he was for sale," he snorts derisively. "I don't usually pay for what I want."

"You'd better be packin', if you aim to talk like 'at and live," I say tersely.

"One way to find out if I'm packin'." The newcomer chuckles and closely watches my reaction before he squints off at the shimmering mirage in the distance.

He looks back down at me. "Name's Rimfire." He extends his hand. I ignore it.

Across the street, a woman picks up her child and scurries behind a growing crowd of curious onlookers that are peering from an alley.

The man who calls himself Rimfire tugs his pant legs up slightly in preparation of sitting down next to me. "You want to move over?" he says.

Without looking up, I unload a jaw of tobacco juice, which lands perilously close to the stranger's dusty boots.

We lock eyes and glare at each other.

A loaded wagon pulls out of the lumberyard across the street. The driver sees us and quickly snaps his whip over the mules. They break into a trot.

"Where'd you say you come from?" I ask the stranger.

"I didn't."

I examine the stranger's hands closely; still wondering where I have seen him before. "Play poker?"

"I reckon."

"Jacks to Open, Spit in the Ocean, or Mexican Sweat?"

"Five Card Draw," he sneers.

The man called Rimfire unloads a stream of amber juice of his own and hits my right boot dead center.

The watching crowd ducks behind a building. A sleeping dog suddenly wakes from his nap in the middle of the street.

He slinks away.

"Where'd you learn to spit like 'at?" I demand.

"Yuma Prison."

Then I remember where I've seen the man before.

I go for my gun.

From behind me, someone grabs my arm with an iron grip.

Startled, I turn and look into a pair of cruel green eyes that fill my heart with terror.

The Bitch/Nurse from Hell!

"There you are, you naughty boy." She smoothes her white uniform and adjusts her 'Shady Rest' marshall's badge. "I've been looking all over for you, hon. It's time for your medication and your bath." She releases the brake on my wheelchair.

"See you later at Canasta?" I ask the tall stranger.

"Nah, I'm meetin' Sarah Jo for Bingo," he says.

"You keep your hands off Sarah Jo!" I demand. "She's my woman."

"Smile when you say that," says the man called Rimfire.

D. CREASON BARTLETT

Sunday Shift

I was seriously thinking of up and quitting working the meat counter when this guy—I swear it was Jesus—walked in, went right past the beer, wine and bread, and turned down the cookie aisle heading straight for me. He had dirty bare feet, long crusty hair with leaves tangled in it, and he had on a bath robe that looked like it came from the Omni Hotel's dumpster. It smelled like it too, I noticed, when he got to the meat counter and stood there staring at the rolls of sausage, the stuffed pork chops stained blood-red with paprika, and the piles of ground round.

Glen, the assistant manager, was in the stockroom eating a cinnamon roll and drinking chocolate milk he'd looted from the shelves. If he saw this Jesus guy, Glen would huff up and down the aisles behind him, spraying Lysol until all the meat tasted like pine bark. Glen wasn't what you'd call righteous. On Sunday afternoons when it was real slow around here, he'd make you do things like pick dead flies out of the bottom of the milk cooler, which was a fine waste of time since you just ended up picking out the same flies over and over. They'd thaw out, come back to life, and fly right back into the cooler. And Glen sure wouldn't help out at the meat counter, even when the after-church rush came in around noon and the line went all the way to the beer section. Let me tell you, that's not a very forgiving crowd.

Which was why I hoped Jesus would be gone by then. They wouldn't like the look of him, and I'd have to hear about it from every one of them. So I asked Jesus if I could help him, and he said—with this voice like he'd gargled with gravel—that he wanted some sliced roast beef. He held out his hand with two nickels and a penny in it. That roast beef was $4.99 a pound, and if there was one thing I knew about slicing that stuff, it was that there's no way to slice eleven cents worth of it. It's the kind of stuff we sliced ourselves for snacks all the time if no one was looking.

But then Glen was looking. He came out from the stockroom and stood at the end of the counter eyeballing Jesus. I tell you, if there was one thing I wanted to do before leaving this world, it was to leave Glen at this meat counter in the middle of the after-church rush. Tell him right there in front of all those accusing eyes that he could clean out the dead flies from the milk cooler himself.

But first I had to get rid of Jesus, who still held out the eleven cents in his hand like an offering. I sliced a piece of roast beef and put it in on the scale. Thirty-three cents for one slice. Glen looked at me, then over at Jesus again. He couldn't see the prices or what I rang up from where he was, but he had his arms folded across his chest and was puffed up in his red butcher's apron like some kind of legionnaire.

I cleared the scale and put in the price of pressed ham, the cheapest stuff we have. The price came up at nine cents. I printed it, wrapped the beef, and handed it to Jesus.

"Pay up front," I said.

"Bless you," he said, looking at the package of meat like it was the Holy Grail. Or maybe what he said was thank you, but you understand what you want to, I guess, and what I understood was that I'd only done that to get him out and to keep Glen off my back.

Jesus went back down the cookie aisle, past the wine and bread and beer, and Glen headed for the chemical aisle. I looked at the clock. About ten minutes before the church-crowd got here. Enough time for the Lysol to clear up, for me to pick a few flies out of the milk cooler, and for things to get back to normal.

31

NANCY BERTONCELJ

Dèjá Vu

It was a dark and stormy night when she walked into the Steak House wearing a short black silk dress that clung to her shapely hips. A mane of sun-gold hair accented her tan skin. She sat beside Brett on the waiting bench and he thought she looked familiar, but decided it was simply dèjá vu.

"How long do you think it'll be?" she asked, an odd expression crossing her face when their eyes met.

"Not long. Don't I know you from somewhere?"

"All the boys say that."

The waiter arrived to announce an available table.

"Why not join me?" Brett was certain now that he had met her before.

After they introduced themselves as Brett and Guinevere, they sat at a table nestled in a corner. Brett ordered the house wine.

The waiter commented, "Excellent choice, Sir."

Brett studied her, noted the long tan legs. "Where did you go to college?" he asked.

"Berkeley."

"I thought I knew you. Maybe I've seen you around campus."

"Perhaps."

"So, what brings you to Houston."

"Plastic surgery. A world famous doctor at the medical center."

"You look perfect as you are. Yes, perfectly beautiful."

"Thank you, but one can never be too perfect."

Her breasts seemed to fall out of her dress, large snow balls.

"Do you want to touch me?" she asked.

Brett gulped and reached across the table, so much in haste he spilled the wine.

"Not now! I didn't mean now."

She stretched her legs on the adjacent chair. Legs. He'd never seen such beautiful legs. Long. The longest legs he'd ever seen.

He looked down at the menu. "So what will it be? I'm a steak and potato man myself."

"I'll have the Caesar salad. I have to watch the calories."

"Soooooo, Guinevere, what do you do in California?"

"I surf. I Rollerblade. I aerobicize."

"Well, that certainly does sound interesting."

"Do you like my legs, Brett?" She separated them slightly a la Sharon Stone.

The waiter dropped a tray of glasses.

"They are the most extraordinary two things I have ever seen?"

"Would you like to make love to me, Brett?"

"That would be nice," he managed to choke out.

"You don't remember, do you?"

"Remember what?"

"The blind date your fraternity set you up with, big night in Hollywood?"

A cloudy patch of the past started to come back. His "brothers" set him up all right. He was to take her to a premiere and out to Spago's where the movie stars hung. But when she'd opened the door, he'd seen the fattest, ugliest girl imaginable. He'd turned and run straight down the palm-lined street. Frat boys giggled in the bushes.

His wine glass splintered.

"Well then," he said, "I guess sex is out?"

Paper Cut to the Soul

Marcia watched Darlene Dalton exhale a cloud of gray smoke, blink a contact lens back in place and wail, "Like a paper cut to the soul!"

Marcia made a quick note. Some of Darlene's phrases were good and, without asking, she had used a few of them in her last self-help book *It's NOT What you Get, It's what you Get Over.* Marcia figured Darlene owed her that much, dropping in between patients for free advice.

"So," Marcia said in her best therapist's voice, "this one didn't work out either?"

"No!" Darlene plucked a blonde hair from her red designer suit. Her wispy voice rose to a whine, "And I still owe Visa for all that wilderness equipment." Popping a breath mint in her mouth, she complained, "You said go where guys are, camping, outdoor stuff, Sierra Club. I did, and what did I find?" Grinding the mint between newly straightened teeth, she huffed, "How to find the can in the dark. You have never seen such dark!"

"That's it?" Marcia, noting a paying appointment was due in ten minutes, needed Darlene out of there. "Tell you what," she said, standing the way she'd learned in Patient Management. "Let's have a drink after work at the bar downstairs. Oh, you have a five-o'clock to show a house?"

Darlene paused before heading to her real estate office down the hall. Fluffing Madonna-styled hair with fingernails matching the vermilion suit, she said, "Be finished by six-thirty. Want to meet then?"

"Sure, nothing else going on." Marcia heaved a sigh as the door closed leaving the scent of Darlene's latest cologne, and pulled the next client's file. Lenny Welch. Dropped and divorced. Says he needs a woman's point of view.

She knew he meant a shoulder to cry on, but she could be whoever, critical parent, abandoning spouse, SOB boss, whatever helped clients get in touch with their pain, uncover their issues.

Lenny Welch edged in, skinny body, round face, horn rimmed glasses and a perpetually surprised expression.

"Come in, Lenny."

"How's it going, Marcia?" Nervous, he rubbed his palms together.

She watched him ease cautiously into the chair like it would bite. "Great day to be alive. What do you think?"

Lenny slapped his leg and cackled. "I like your attitude, Marcia. Down to earth. Perceptive." He went on schmoozing, hoping, she knew, for an easy session. Most people resist change. With Lenny it was a mission.

"Let's get started, Lenny. Meter's running."

He let out another cackle before leaning forward, clearing his throat, Adams' apple bobbing. "I called her today," he said, misty eyed.

"Why d'you do that, Lenny?" Training kept impatience from her voice. "That's acting like a wimp. The more you crawl, the more Susan runs away. We've been down this road."

She listened to his rationalizations, excuses, apologies, wishing she were back in her skimpy costume, serving drinks, pocketing tips, tending bar. She had worked her way through school and couldn't wait to finish, to open an office. Now here she was, doing her best with Lenny, a nice guy, but. And down the hall from Darlene. If only—no, it would be unethical to set them up. She worked too hard for her license. But it had been a long day and she did something desperate. "Lenny, you had any dates since Susan jumped ship?"

"No! Susan might change her mind. I want to be available."

Marcia checked herself before rolling her eyes. Too bad. They were perfect for each other. They could whine in unison. No, she busted her buns to get here, wouldn't jeopardize the license.

They got through the forty-five minutes, Lenny firing excuses, Marcia blocking them like hockey pucks.

She glanced at the clock.

Lenny looking relieved, pulled out his checkbook.

"Thank you, Lenny. Same time next week?"

He jumped to his feet like he was getting out of detention. "Yeah," he crowed. "I feel so much better."

After he left, she smoked one cigarette from the pack Darlene left. Last patient due in ten minutes. Work up the notes from today, and look forward to that drink.

The bar was cool, dark, soft music. Marcia squared her shoulders, sucked in her breath, and smoothed her skirt. Yeah, she could still wear the skimpy uniform.

Weaving her way between tables to the bar, a nice looking guy stood up, said he recognized her from her former occupation. "Sorry," she told him, "I'm meeting someone."

Then she heard it. The cackle and right behind it the wispy voice rising in a whine. She stopped, stared across the bar wondering how, when? Lenny and Darlene, their heads together. He, lighting her cigarette like he was Humphrey Bogart. Darlene, exhaling.

Behind the veil of smoke Marcia heard her say, ". . . like a paper cut to the soul." The whine duet started.

"Yeah," Marcia said to the dude from her old job. "I d love to join you for a drink."

SHARON ECKERT-BOSWELL

Little Palm Island

It's four o'clock in the afternoon at Little Palm Island off the coast of the Florida Keys. Javier is working here but I haven't seen him yet. The last time we met was in Mexico City fifteen years ago, although it seems like only yesterday.

I sit on the deck of my thatched-roof bungalow—my feet propped up on the cypress and bamboo railing–and watch a tiny finch light on an air root hanging from a banyan tree and then fly away. In the distance a small fishing boat glides past carrying supplies to the neighboring mangrove-bordered ait. Could he be on that boat? His handsome Latin face flashes across my mind. Will I recognize him now? It was all so long ago, yet the pain and the anger have taken permanent residence in my soul. "Ah, Latin lovers," they say. "Aren't they all the same?" But I know for a fact that some are more heartless than others.

I look toward the pier where boats from the mainland dock and pelicans perch atop the high posts that frame the wooden decking. Out of sight, a baggage cart drives by making crunching sounds on the gravel-covered walking path. Someone is checking in. A greeter hawks the island's amenities: "Tonight there will be musical entertainment and a seven-course meal will be served in the open-air dining room."

That voice—the accent. My heart jumps.

I move indoors. The coolness of my room and the whirring sound of the ceiling fan calm me. No—it's not time yet.

I pick up the flyer that was slipped under the door and read: "This evening our resident Latin troubadour, Javier Hidalgo, will be taking requests for your favorite songs."

I let the paper flutter to the floor and enter the bedroom.

What will I wear tonight? Yes, the sleeveless linen dress will be fine and the Mexican silver pendant. The words inscribed on the back have long since burned themselves into my memory: *Angélica, mi querida, mi único amor, I will love you forever, Javier.*

And I will carry the raffia purse with the twisted rope shoulder strap that I purchased today from the quaint little shop on the island. Inside the purse I'll place my song request signed: *Tu querida, tu único amor, Angélica*–and the small mother of pearl pistol.

ANN REISFELD BOUTTE

The Hummingbird

Hours after the family hung the feeder, the hummingbird appeared. It soared over the backyard fence, swooped through the garden and rose to the red plastic flowerets where it hovered and sipped. Occasionally, between precision flights, it perched on the rim, its green fluorescent feathers reflecting sun. Dwarfed by the sparrows, finches and doves at the larger wild bird feeder, it was a study of grace and power in miniature. But this morning, it lies broken on the wooden deck, its tiny wings, once a blur of movement, pressed close to its body.

The family, with shoulders and spirits drooping, stands gazing down at the bird. Mother blames herself for cultivating the garden. Last spring, she planted pink and white impatiens, plumbago with light blue blossoms, and purple bougainvillea. She is certain the flowers, particularly the burst of magenta that scales the trellis along the fence, drew the hummingbird to their yard.

Father says, no, the blame is his. The night before he moved the grill out of a drizzling rain from its usual location to a place under the eave where the feeder hung. He surmises that the bird, in the swale of its flight, crashed into the grill, snapping its fragile, scarlet neck.

Daughter claims her share of the burden. She moved the feeder to a hook nearer the kitchen window, allowing for a better view and setting the bird up for its fatal plunge.

In a next-door window, a Cheshire cat grin spreads across thirteen-year-old Charlie's face as he watches the family lay the bird in a tissue-lined box and place it in the ground. Then, carefully, he wraps his slingshot in a kerchief and tucks it in the corner of a drawer.

ROBERTA PIPES BOWMAN

You Don't Say

It is time for another visit from Bill Watson. I see him coming down the lane raising puffs of dust after each step. I set out cold drinks. Today, I have been thinking of Indians who lived on this farm and wondering what they were like. Sometimes I plow up an arrow chip and put it in a box. Maybe Bill would know more stories about them.

He does. "Yes, my folks came to Texas with a wagon train after the Civil War. I guess they wanted a change after all those hard, bitter times. When they crossed Red River, they drove into bluebonnets up to the axles of ox-drawn wagons. It was like driving straight into the ocean. Never had they seen anything so beautiful. Blue stem grass was shoulder high."

"Now, there's just a clump here and there." I remarked.

"That's right. They thought it was almost heaven. That night they camped by a little creek with plenty of water, grass, and game. It was so peaceful they had no fear. They were far away from landlords, taxes, and worn out land. Cousin Will, my Aunt Helda's youngest boy, was not feeling well. Aunt Helda made him a pallet under a tree and she decided to sleep nearby. Folks said she always put on a white nightgown and white cap to sleep in regardless, on the trail or home."

"That must have been nice, sleeping under the stars, clean air, quiet, just the night birds making little cheeps,." I said and thought of my camping times with crowded grounds, mosquitoes. Other campers often made so much racket it seemed like downtown.

"They had night birds all right but they couldn't fly. Aunt Helda was half-awake when she heard the first bird call. She thought it was a strange bird and didn't remember ever hearing one like that. They were told all Indians were on reservations and once in a while a raiding party might come down but only farther west. A sudden yell startled Aunt Helda. She jumped up in her white nightgown and saw an Indian with a tomahawk ready to strike

Cousin Will. She screeched, raised her arms, made the sign of the cross and started speaking in a weird, hissing tongue. The Indian stopped, turned pale, dropped the tomahawk and ran as if all the demons of hell were after him."

"Did anybody ever find out what she said to make him run?"

Bill shuffled his chair around and sipped on the drink. He wiped his mouth and answered, "Not right away. You see folks in the wagon train'd been robbed on the trip and robbers took their weapons. The money was hidden but there was no place to buy guns. It was a terrible, frightful time. Somebody thought Helda was speaking Comanche, but she probably didn't know any. Before she died she told

Cousin Will she turned herself into a rattlesnake and threatened that Indian with eternal torment if he didn't run."

"Hmmm," I said and thought of an Indian and snake story I knew. Maybe I'd tell Bill that tale the next time he came by. Meanwhile, I asked him if he'd like to walk around the place and look at the hay crop.

MICHAEL BRACKEN

Better to Have Loved

The 747 carrying Samantha disappeared into the clouds while I watched from a window inside the terminal. After the plane had been out of sight nearly ten minutes, I turned away and began the long walk back through the terminal to the garage where I'd left my car.

The scent of her perfume still clung to my clothes and the waxy taste of her cherry red lipstick still clung to my lips. If I closed my eyes I saw her there before me, honey-blonde hair framing her oval face, a pair of pale blue eyes staring back at me without remorse. It's been said that parting is such sweet sorrow, but it's much more than that. Parting is the realization that everything you once shared is little more than a slowly fading memory.

As I approached my car, I pressed the electronic device in my pocket, deactivating the auto-alarm. Then I unlocked the door and slid behind the wheel. Instead of bringing the engine to life, I gripped the steering wheel tightly with each hand and leaned my forehead against it, waiting for tears that wouldn't come.

She'd made all her plans without me, had told each of her friends of her decision, had packed her bags and had them waiting in the closet before confronting me with the news of her impending departure.

Samantha had reasons for leaving me, reasons that she spelled out in great detail after she made slow, sweet, delicate love to me for the final time. I tried to convince her to stay, used every argument I could think of, and made every promise that I thought might cause her to change her mind, but nothing did.

At the airport, after learning her flight number, I redoubled my effort, if not for her to stay, then at least for her to take a later flight. I wanted her to remain with me as long as possible, but when the airline announced boarding, she stood, gathered her carry-on luggage in one hand, and stretched up to kiss me for the last time.

I grabbed her, wrapping my thick fingers around her upper arm through the rough wool of her sweater. She glared at me then.

"It's too late," she said as she jerked away. "I'm going home."

I wanted to tell her to stay and I wanted to tell her why, but I couldn't. Instead, I watched her board the plane.

I banged my forehead against the steering wheel one time, wondering if there was any other way I could have prevented her from taking that flight, and realized there was nothing else I could have done without attracting unwanted attention.

Perhaps if I had known Samantha's plans, I could have altered the chain of events set in motion months earlier. But I hadn't.

Two hours after her plane leveled off on its trip across the Atlantic toward Dublin, it would explode. Somewhere across town Sean would phone one of the news services and claim credit on behalf of our organization.

After straightening in my seat, I wiped at my eyes with the tips of my fingers. Then I started my car, slipped it into gear, and backed out of the parking space.

I loved Samantha and would always remember what we had shared, but the organization was my life and would never abandon me the way she had.

MARTHA BRANIFF

Tula's Bedroom

Tula took *los hombres* by the hand, and the women too—all the lonely people. She led them to her bedroom up a winding staircase of an old adobe building in the barrio. No one ever felt unloved, even though they paid her to make the angels sing.

Fertile Virgin, Maria de Guadelupe, flooded Tula's bedroom with roses and watched over her, saved her from *mal ojo,* envy eyes of spiteful ones who hated Tula's caramel skin, raven mane, heavy lashes over night-eyes.

Lizards sunned her window, scampered over bougainvillea: orange, shock-red, magenta. And brown chameleons turned lime-green in the shadow of *el sol,* while roosters in the yard strutted to the rhythmic moans of joy from Tula's lovers.

On starry nights, I would ascend Tula's stairway, stroke her tresses on the altar of crisp white sheets. Pigs danced in their pens below us, as she held my body like the Pieta and stroked my hair like the Madre de Dios touched the bleeding body of Jesu Christo.

No one could explain how the fire started. Some believed it was the heart, *el corazon,* of her lover consumed in blazon ecstasy. Others said it was the thousand candles Tula lit before the Virgin, before moving magic fingers to play her lover's body.

In the ashes of her bedroom, charred boards and cracked adobe, I cried with all the people, while lizards, pigs and roosters sniffed the holy ruins. Men and women searched with fleshed out fingers for bones from her body. We placed her relics on our altars, kissed the marrow with salted tears and prayed to become like Santa Tula, to make the angels sing.

ELIZABETH BRATTEN

Outpost Near the Sam Houston Toll Way

As I speed along the tollway, I watch for the pigeons. I like to think the fitful flock, perched on high tension lines waits for me. Powered down, with wings retracted, or feathers ruffled by a probing breeze, all heads incline toward the traffic flowing south. The vagabonds are gray-blue, white or pearl, some milky brown with purple breasts. A measured space separates each squatter. A quick flutter, and the line restructures. Each bird claims its station. I search for a cause. Why do the wanderers choose this particular roost? Is it an observation post, or a pause for an audience with the sun? Can an attitude of light, or weight of air hold them, poised and steady in the wind? I consider avian instinct, or a convivial meeting ground. They remain—wrapped and riveted on pigeon-pink feet—a fixture against the sky. The song of the wire, or the lure of territory could attract and hold. What of the sky, with its moving hardware, or clouds, forecasting rain? I am surprised each time I pass to find them, staying put. I go far to find a reason for this solitary stop. Calm or wild the wind they rock and I drive on, with the puzzle unsprung.

ARLENE WHITE-BRISCO

Christmas Dinner

The table is laden with more food than it is designed to hold. Every inch covered with overstuffed bowls and platters. The chatter of three generations of family fills the small two-story, colonial home. Everyone is there; all five siblings with their respective spouses and a herd of grandchildren. Unsolicited confessions of "I haven't eaten all day," are given as justifications to pilfer tidbits of food before dinner.

The meal starts with the scurrying to obtain a seat at the table. But, like the nursery game of musical chairs, there are never enough and the losers must obtain other chairs from upstairs or the garage. The older grandchildren assert their entry into adulthood by insisting on sitting at the main table instead of the adjacent children's table. After all are seated, Grandpa and Nana take their places at each end of the table and look up with pride at their family.

Usually, the simultaneous passing and scarfing down of food follow a quick grace. But this Christmas is different. Everyone—thinking this could be the last of such dinners— takes an extra moment to acknowledge God and silently ask for his continued blessings on the family. Two months earlier, Grandpa had informed the family that he had been diagnosed with an advanced stage of prostate cancer.

During dinner, Grandpa grows so weak that he excuses himself, refusing all offers of assistance. The little-ones are shocked that he would leave before dessert. "Why you leaving, Grandpa?" a four-year-old granddaughter asks. "Have you been put in time-out again?"

Her innocent humor brings a smile to his face and he kisses the top of her head. This makes all the rest at the children's table whine for the same. Grandpa lovingly bestows each a kiss before inching his way up the stairs. Had it not been for the comforting hugs from the stronger members of the family, those around the table who hadn't learned to hide their emotions would have been in tears.

The meal always ends with the family's rendition of the *Twelve Days of Christmas*. Each person is secretly assigned a day by drawing from a baseball cap. The person with the fifth day—hopefully someone who can't hold a tune—is assured to be the butt of jokes for the rest of the evening. This year, the usually jovial sing-along is blanketed by a solemnness as everyone pretends not to be upset by the absence of Grandpa. Each member half-heartedly belts out his solo at the revealing moment.

Reaching the part of the fifth day, the family looks around wanting to know who is the unlucky sap. There is a short silence, then a faint but distinctive, "Fiiive Goldeeen Riings," crackles down the stairs.

"Grandpa," everyone laughs. The evening fills with lasting memories. When surrounded by family that loves you even the bleakest moments are bearable.

JEANNETTE BROWN

Correcting Obsession

As she sits in The Modern Beauty Shoppe awaiting her manicure, Beverly corrects the typo on page 34 of the novel she is reading. Earlier, scanning the morning paper, she had circled three incorrect noun/verb agreements and a subhead that read "Their moving off center on zoning decision." Yesterday, she underlined the names of publications in *Newsweek* that were in plain type but should have been italicized. She also connected compound phrases that have become one word.

Beverly had quit her job as a magazine editor when she realized that details were overtaking the more important elements such as context and style. Now correcting the details is merely a hobby. Her new job, writing computer manuals, is renowned for being inexact, for creating stick sentences that might not contain a noun. At the office, she feels deliciously criminal.

Details not in print fail to catch her notice. She simply cannot see her uneven hem, a button hanging by a thread, a run in her hose. Her friends think her messy, blowzy, but they love her for not pointing out their *faux pas*. They mistake her myopia for forgiveness.

Beverly does not question the motives of the female colleague who gave her the manicure gift certificate at the Christmas party.

At the nail table, Beverly reads the labels on the bottles of polish, mouthing the candy-color names: Peppermint Pink, Caramel Red, Lemon Drop Yellow. They make her salivate. She can't find any errors.

Beverly yelps when the manicurist draws blood, a bright red globlette where the cuticle had been. As the manicurist wipes the blood with the towel lying under her splayed fingers,

48

Beverly doesn't notice the other spots—blood and polish and chemicals for fixing mistakes. She doesn't notice the manicurist returning the cuticle clippers to a drawer instead of the blue sterilizer.

Several months later, Beverly does notice her fever, her tiredness, and her increasingly yellow eyes. She listens carefully to her doctor, goes home, and marks the typos in the literature that describes the symptoms and treatment for hepatitis B.

Her failing liver needs bed rest. She fluffs up her pillows and assembles an impressive stack of novels and magazines. She puts a dozen red-ink pens in a cup on the nightstand. After a few weeks, she ceases to stalk errors.

Beverly never sees the typos in her obit.

A Lady Undone

I don't suppose anyone ever called her beautiful, but perhaps when she was newly arrived on the scene, all painted and bejeweled, some might have called her small and pretty, especially when compared to her more opulent neighbor.

The years passed. Unkind years at best. She aged ungracefully, no longer dipping into the rouge pot, no longer adorned by even the cheapest jewels. Now she simply looks worn-out, unkempt, even abused, this town in Texas they call Pasadena.

Why?

Dear Lord, why'd I have to be the first born? The only one with breasts? Why'd You send him to my bed? Under my covers? Why'd You let him do all them things to me? Send me so much hurt?

Ah! The pleasure part. Them beggin' and pleadin', willing to do anything. Just like some old hound dog sniffin' and scratchin' at my Mama's backdoor.

I spread my legs and say: Gimme a quarter. Gimme me a dollar. Gimme me fifty for a new red dress. Snuggle up close to them gentlemens and whisper real sweet, Sugar, if I had a few thousand, I'd buy me a shiny black Corvette.

Them saying: Sure, honey. Anything for you. Meaning anything for *it*.

All them daddies want what I got.

BILLIE LOU CANTWELL

In the Woods

In the winter, land was cleared in the woods and in its center the little house was under construction. Simmering stumps and resin scent of fresh cut trees permeated as November leant her autumn burst of turning leaves. I remember best those damp afternoons when snappy air bit my nose, made it moist and pink. Huddled in a blue blanket, I sat on a stump to watch mom and dad saw trees, axe through brush, and laugh at their efforts. I listened raptly to the saw's grind through sweet gum trunks, to the warning crack of timber giving up with a slow-motion keel to the leafy sea of earth, sighing a final, holy breath as branches brushed the air, other trees, the ground. I held my own breath while a moment of tingling silence riveted, before the shudder of leaves, twigs, and insects nestled on unfamiliar ground. I scurried from my blanket burrow to feel the new stump, wanting to be the first to touch what had forever been hidden, to find the wood cool, dense. I ran a finger through the sap, touched it to my tongue and grinned as the flat-tasting resin warmed. The sweet gum's stickiness was instant. I knew I would hate the gum—rough on my teeth, but it was part of the event. The cold day, the quiet wood, the new house played in all our minds. In those piney woods, love danced to the music of the woods while we claimed our future. My mother, my father, myself. Happy. Not a rare knowledge when one is three.

KRISTI CASSIN

Day of the Dead

Let's make Dad his own *offrenda,* your children say, seeking
answers, ways to unload pain. You know, the way they do in
Mexico, they say, looking at me hopefully. And I succumb,
fearing fresh hurt and thwarted expectations. We each get three
choices to put on the altar, with Mom's the last, they say,
already busy in deliberation. I watch them scatter petals on
your bureau, forming paths of orange and brilliant scarlet,
chrysanthemum and coxcomb, a bed of memory. Your bureau,
once your bailiwick, now in a new space in the empty guest
room. Repository for moments captured, fleeting time, altar
of lost identity. Your children place their objects one by one
with care, fashioning a phoenix from your ashes, cold these
long years. Well-chewed pipe, gold watch still intact, gold
pen and pencil set worn with use and time. High school signet
ring, yellowed diplomas framed in austere black, law school
honors listed, wooden gavel from your days at court. The key
to your first office, embalmed in lucite square. Plastic model
of your high-rise office building—your home away from
home. Your last. Photos in the background—your children
playing soccer, singing in the choir, graduating, your arms
around them, smiling. Our wedding picture, faded, propped
on top of prayer book. For the final offering I place your silver
cross and chain, refrain from adding to your bier an empty
bottle and spent cartridge.

JUNE SHORT CHALON

The Man With Two Magnolias

Elderly Ambrose knew all about old mother magnolia tree, especially those wicked, worrisome things Mam Tree had witnessed for more than a hundred years in mistress's garden on Bayou St. John Road. Ambrose—his ancestors beyond memory—worked for the Rousseaux family with no complaints. He had cared for their boy Roger since he was a toddler. He truly loved Roger, but there were times when he thought Roger was possessed by Mam. The child was drawn to the tree's lustrous rich green leaves, their velvety undersides; the creamy white flowers that perfumed the air before they gave way to pineapple-shaped cones that spat forth oily-feeling, Chinese-red seeds. Roger carried the seeds by the pocketful and habitually planted them on the family property. With each seed, came Ambrose's warning about old Mam.

When the paddle wheeler Laura Lee sounded its Fourth of July sailing, it greeted Roger's twentieth birthday, and also punctuated his final farewell to New Orleans. Toting potted magnolia saplings, Ambrose pleaded with Roger not to take the trees. As Roger ascended the gangplank, Ambrose sobbed, "Ol' Mam g'wan be some mad 'bout de babes g'wan!" As a child Roger had overheard confusing, scary bits attributed to Mam Tree and various family members, but for some reason he always felt secure when sheltered by Mam's huge boughs. He had dismissed Ambrose's superstitions and those horrible stories. Now, he recalled the tale of how Mam was brought south as a seedling by his mother's relatives. He envisioned two, even more, imposing magnolias for his Caddo Lake plantation.

For Roger's centennial anniversary, an exceptional celebration was planned: a feast, festivities, and fireworks! Roger's fortunes far surpassed those of his youthful dreams.

The two magnolias—their trunks now larger than his body—were splendid specimens. They were legendary. Flags and lanterns adorned his adored magnolias, and bunting edged the lower and upper galleries of the house. Roger arose early. Peering out, two disturbing things caught his attention—a fierce storm raged in the western sky, and between his magnolias, stood two costumed ladies wildly gesturing to an ancient black man. Suddenly, a slashing swirl of magnolia limbs seemed to sweep them away. A huge bolt of lightning struck a mortal blow to the slightly taller tree; it fell, deforming the other. Roger felt a distinct chill; he wondered how he could bear the loss of his beloved trees.

Roger edged back to his bed. Head in hands, he pondered his grandmother, mother, and kindly old Ambrose. Roger knew what he had to do. Time was precious. He ordered the two trees harvested and shipped east for special milling. On All Hallows Eve, Roger, with last year's remaining seed in his suit pocket, was buried between the two rotting stumps in his elaborately carved magnolia coffin.

BETH LYNN CLEGG

Beholden to None

She knew her seventy-three-year-old body like she knew every dead-end and fork in the red dirt roads that twisted and turned through the East Texas forest where she, and ancestors before her—going back more than three hundred years— cleared land, planted crops and raised families. She could butcher a hog, pick off a rabbit on the run at a hundred yards with a single shot, or catch a mess of crappie from the pond, to put food on the table. She'd plow and plant an acre of vegetables in the morning. Mend fences, put up preserves, or tend flowerbeds in the afternoon.

It took several leg surgeries to clear out clogged arteries, still, she didn't take kindly to a doctor telling her to eat healthy, stop smoking, and get more rest. Hire someone to do the chores, or let her boys take over, he'd said. But the boys had their own families, only visited when they could, and she didn't cotton to being beholden to anyone. She gave it a try for a spell, but it didn't last. She'd beaten TB, raised three sons, buried two husbands, and had a deep, abiding faith in the hereafter. She knew her life would never be the same, so what was the point to living another twenty years if some fool doctor had taken away most all of her every-day pleasures.

She washed up the dishes from a supper of fried pork chops, collard greens, and 'taters with cream gravy, poured a cup of strong black coffee, and lit up a L&M. Inhaling deeply, she leaned back in the recliner as smoke escaped in perfect circles to rise above her head.

JACK CRUMPLER

Beauty

Their temporal elusiveness is part of their beauty, those vignettes of nature—a scatter of twinkling sparkles flung across the lake's waters by a late winter afternoon's sun and teased by a playful wind. The mesmerizing hues of a double rainbow hang in the west after morning rain. A flower's exquisite, colorful intricacy fades as it makes seeds to give us next season's wondrous bouquet. The cold white of a full moon is carved and shaped like a Halloween jack-o-lantern by tatters of wind-blown clouds, an ever-changing game of heavenly hide-and-seek. Venus shimmers in the barely-dark November sky, just light enough for the moving V formation of honking geese to show itself in silhouette. After the flood, a host of frogs croak out a lively cacophony of sounds that blend into a haunting throb of harmonics. A dewy morning strings pearls of wetness on a spider's web, vaporous jewelry destined to evaporate in the day's heat. Or is it the Earth's antenna to receive signals from the spirit in the sky? A single drop of water hangs on the pine needle's tip, refracting sunlight into a gem worthy of its sylvan setting. Dawn fires the morning clouds, kindles embers among their froth before the rising sun extinguishes the fiery show of its own making. A vibrant dot of red, a male cardinal, brightens the gray-green forest, dulled by the rainy day's wetness. White, pure as only nature can present, radiates from the gliding gull and the still-as-stone great egret, poised to snatch a fish. Some of these beauties are too far away to be touched. Others move as we move, putting themselves forever out of our grasp. If touched, some vanish, slain by the admiring hand that would hold them. Nevertheless, glimpses of beauty live, and others like them will live again. 'Tis a wonderful thing about beauty: For those who will see, it never dies, testimony to infinity's promise.

JACK CRUMPLER

The Nearby Diner

"**W**elcome to the Nearby Diner, bubba," he said, took my order for iced tea, came back with it promptly and introduced himself as he served it. "I'm Dideon, owner of the joint. First trip to Nearby?"

I nodded as I sipped the tea.

With a jerking thumb motion to his left, he asked, "Staying at the Gateview Inn?"

"Yes." I spun on the backless counter stool to glance at the Pearly Gates across the street. There was no activity so I turned to face Dideon. The smell of something cooking tempted me to order a burger, but I didn't.

He plucked the toothpick from his mouth and asked, "Trying to get in there?"

"Yes. Didn't think it'd take so long to get here or be so warm. That's why I stopped in for something to drink."

"No need to rush." He rubbed the counter with a tattered white hand towel.

"Quite a location you've got, just across the street from Heaven." I surveyed the floor-to-ceiling picture windows. All of the booths next to them were empty. "Where is everybody?"

"Slow day for some reason," Dideon answered. I nodded toward the gates. "What's the drill? Do they open automatically when you walk up to 'em?"

"Nah. You ring a bell. Saint Peter answers. He has a computer terminal on a pedestal just inside the gate. Tell him your name, he enters the data and sees if you pass muster. If not, he goes away. If you do pass, he opens the gate and lets you in. That's when the fun begins."

"Fun?"

"Yeah. Sometimes when a person moseys up to the gate, people materialize from out of nowhere, trying to get in. Some of 'em been trying for God only knows how long."

I frowned.

"They believe it demonstrates their commitment to Heavenly beliefs and such. Peter doesn't buy it, though. Has a pack of Rottweilers to keep 'em out if they get unruly."

I twisted and looked outside briefly. "What are all those tables and tents out there?"

"Places for vendors. They sell all sorts of stuff—tracts, tapes, holy water, halos, wings, you name it. Some guy sells a balm named 'AnGel' that he claims will get you in. Doesn't. Another claims to be a computer hacker. Says for fifty bucks he can change the heavenly record. Can't."

"You seem to know a lot about it. Have you been here long?"

"Yeah."

"Have you tried to get in?"

"Oh, I can go in and out as I please. The diner, Gateview Inn and all those vending spaces are operated under concessions granted by Heaven. I run the diner so I can help people like you when you show up."

"Help? How?"

"Information. Good food and service. Fair prices. Sympathetic ear. Stuff like that." Dideon cocked his head as if listening to something. "'Bout to get busy. Seven-forty-seven crashed into an office building near the Dallas Airport. A big disaster in a Bible Belt location always churns up lots of business." He pointed outside. "See?"

I turned on my stool to see the street full of people. A crowd had gathered at the Pearly Gates.

"That's Saint Peter, the big old dude in the dingy white beard, wearing denim bib overalls and the St. Louis Rams hat."

I watched as Peter listened to an older man, then checked the computer. Peter shook his head and the man left.

"Ah! See there," Dideon said. "That one's on the outs. No heavenly hosts and such for that bubba."

The third person to petition for entry was allowed in, but the waiting crowd was orderly. No one tried to dart through the gate.

"Docile crowd today. Plane crash or a tornado or big explosion takes some of the spizarinctum out of 'em. But they'll get antsy as time goes on." Dideon refilled my tea glass. "When're you going to see about getting in?"

I shrugged. "Like you said, no rush. Tomorrow." I sipped the tea. "Maybe."

"Got your doubts, huh?"

"Well, you never know for sure."

Dideon laughed. "You got that right, bubba. Besides, tonight is chicken 'n dumplings, all you can eat for four-ninety-five, drink included. You wouldn't want to miss that, now, would you?"

CAROLYN A. DAHL

Cutting Cloth for Rag Rugs

Dresses bloom like summer zinnias in the rummage-sale clothes my grandmother presses to her chest. I sit at her feet, still child-blonde, holding tiny scissors to cut clothes to rags for handwoven rugs.

Grandmother lifts the bundle above her head, lets it drop so the clothes fall slowly. I think she holds them in the air with her eyes, large and blue under glasses thick as creek-ice. One-by-one she brings down a skirt, a dress, pants, a blouse. A scarf she catches in mid-air.

She calls me *Stina* in Swedish. I believe the name means love, like how she pulls a man's shirt toward her by its arms, or invites me to dip sweet sugar lumps in coffee she boils with eggshells for clarity and color.

We sit on last year's shaggy rugs, her flashing blades snip open a coat's underarm seam. With practiced hand, she flattens the cloth, cuts it into strips, winds its former life into a tight ball. "You can take off the jewelry," she says. I pull a pretty dress from the pile by its hem, lay it before me like Christmas, red taffeta with gold button balls marking ribs. I count snaps, hooks and eyes, the metal-toothed zipper smiling on its way down the spine.

I cover my body with the dress, compare waists to measure how far I've yet to grow to become what I imagine a woman is. I want to try on lives, slip my skinny identity into others' sleeves, lose childhood in the folds of a woman's party dress, heady with spicy perfume. I hope my grandmother won't mind, if today I don't cut apart the woman I want to become.

CHERYL L. DANIEL

Childhood Room

The windows, tall and narrow, loomed cathedral-like floor to ceiling. Frosty in winter and dusty in summer, they made a sparse barrier from the elements. Facing the pecan mott, they were the eyes of the middle room in our shotgun farmhouse, built in the boom months of 1929. In my mind I see the room huge, but time would surely shrink it, as time does childhood icons. Two iron bedsteads and a footed oak dresser filled it up.

Fabric-backed wallpaper thinly masked the rough tongue-and-groove plank walls. Faded pink chrysanthemums climbed the latticework design on the paper. Deservedly faded, they were thirty years old when I, a child of six, lay sunken in one feather bed, counting the blossoms again and again through the chills and fever of Asian flu. My father was a heap of moaning humanity under Grandma's Texas Star quilt in the other bed. For eight days, we helped each other suffer while Mother and Grandma answered our complaints with swift attention. Keeping vigil, hands wringing aprons, they took temperatures with alcohol-laced thermometers, brewed pots of chicken soup and dumplings, and changed fever-soaked bed linen. Plied with Robitussin, we languished in the incense of Vicks Vaporub on soft, chest plasters of stove-warmed undershirts. I thought being sick was the hard part.

The roses painted on the white porcelain knob spun, as the flat-paneled door squeaked, announcing the spectral entrance of Mother and Grandmother bearing trays blanketed with white, gauzy tea towels. Beneath the towels awaited the lady or the tiger: A cup of warm creamy sweet milk cocoa, or a dose of god-awful black elixir just a shade sweeter than pine tar, that would forever stain the sight of those faded, pink chrysanthemums with its bitter taste.

RHEA DANIEL

Where I'm From

I am from my daddy's drunken heart, beating so fast as though flung from a furious circle of women who are welcoming the men back from the hunt. I am from my mother's matted eyes. My mother, a lil' orphan girl who often was told, step back, black! You too po'. My mother, who cried out, I have my sister to love. My mother, who beat up the world to protect me. I am from my cousin Cora's womb, which wasted away, but only after seven babies grew into children who lived in a ditch to escape the streets and ate out of garbage cans. I am from the Son of God, the Mother Hen of the world. Careening down a dark alley, I run into myself, leopard legs, little streaks. I am from the Yoakum Chaparral Chalet, covered in chicken grease and bathing in a washtub. I am from Jasper, Texas, grasping my knuckles into the cement as I am dragged to death. I am from music, Stravinsky's "Rite of Spring" and Ellington's "Catch the A Train." I am from gardens, honeysuckled and herbed, growing health and healing. I am from nerves, stressed, tired and tangled. I am from the hospital today where I watch my dad's eyes grow big and his body shrink. I watch my mother skate into the room nodding and dreaming. I am from the bottom of the Atlantic, screaming Holocaust, hundreds of thousands of dead bones chilled and cried out, murderer, thief, betrayer. I am from the eighteen hundred block of Isabella in Houston's Third Ward where Mr. Evans used to sit on his porch and nod and Mrs. Turner used to sit on her porch and talk, and everybody said, "Hello, how ya been doing?"

ROYCE DAVIDSON

Houses

"**D**o you really want to know what it's like? Do you?"

"Yes, I do."

"All right then. I'll tell you exactly how it is. It's like a new custom-built house. On the outside, all the colors blend with simple elegance and make the first impression striking. The fresh paint, a sickly sweet, invigorating smell in the air, heightens the newness of the house. From all angles, its symmetry is breathtaking – angles that no one would guess could be put together with such grace and beauty.

"On the inside, the wet bar is nestled in the corner, discreet, yet accessible. All the lights are located right where you expect them to be. The dining room chandelier sparkles with just the right amount of light so as to not intrude on everything else. Perfection. Perfection is what I'm talking about here. Do you understand what I'm talking about?"

"Yes, I do. But . . ."

"No. No buts. Wait before you reply. Wait until I've told you everything about how it is. If the house is custom-built, it's going to last for a long time.

"The only thing is, after a while, that paint will chip. Eventually, the house will need a new coat. And no matter how many coats you put on, it will never have that same smell—sickly sweet, yet invigorating. And after several years of looking at those same angles—that perfect symmetry— they're no longer breathtaking, graceful or beautiful. They're just angles.

"On the inside is where the cracks really start to show. On the inside is where you see it. Creeping along the ceiling, cracks reveal the age and fragility of the house. The roof over your head that has protected you isn't as safe as you think it is.

"Slowly, like the pace and patience of time, when you least expect it, old age will consume the house. But the consumption is never all at once. It's just one thing after another.

"All those fancy amenities that were so wonderful when you first moved into the house, those are an inconvenience now. Crisp gold and brown spirits of feel-good liquid that once filled the wet bare are now not quite so good. The taste is lost. Only the pain lingers. That chandelier is way too bright in the kitchen. Way too bright in the dining room even, where dinners are spent, head down, hovering over your food, not talking.

"Yes, if you go outside and look from a distance, the house still looks good. But only as you move closer do you find out how it truly is. It is imperfect. And there's nothing you can do about it."

BETTY DAVIS

Good Deeds and Bad Acts

My good deeds and bad acts overlap like the binding and edges of a quilt. They must be squirming, shrinking, crawling from each other, not wanting to be seen together, yet, clinging together on a level deep inside, afraid to face the world alone.

Unless I achieve freedom from fear, I cannot be totally bad nor thoroughly good. A swirled pudding of vanilla and chocolate, my good and bad, hold tightly to each other. I am this mixture because I am afraid to be alone, even while I swear God is always with me.

One thing I know, when I have no human being's love, I understand loneliness. Then my life is like the place where day overlaps night, creating dawn and dusk, maybe leaving a glimpse of great good at high noon or a shadow of eclipsed evil in the dead of night.

BETTY DAVIS

Second Base/Second Bed

We gather on the softball field. The park around us is exploding in greens and yellows; daffodils and narcissus are brightly blooming. A soft breeze musses our hair. Our dress is comfortable for practice. One large-busted woman wears a tube top and tight shorts, another wears an oversized T-shirt over shorts that do not show, and still another tall, thin girl wears huge, baggy pants and a halter. Each of us carries a softball glove. One girl wears on her hand a bulky, round glove. We all know what position she wants.

Sitting on the grass, we tell family stories and jokes until Coach comes striding across the field with his clipboard and bag of equipment. "Don't get up," he says. "I want to talk to you."

Today we know some of us will not make the team. I am twenty years older than most of the women, so my chances are slim, but the enjoyment of practicing with the team has made me happy. The outcome makes no difference. I am pleasantly surprised when Coach announces I will play second base.

"Congrats, Grandma," a teenager says.

Another young woman throws her glove down and shrugs. The chosen team takes the field and since they are there, the rest of the women will bat first as they challenge us in practice. We have a good pitcher who quickly retires the other team.

"Way to go, Pitch," the team chants in unison.

Coach looks at me and says, "Come on, you lead off."

I am not a heavy hitter, but almost always get on base. My bat connects with the third pitch. The low fly just clears the hands of their second baseman, and I am on base. The next two batters walk. I am full of myself, so I lead off third base with confidence. The fourth batter hits to shortstop who fumbles, but gets off a good throw. I am already running. I have to slide, but I am going to make it. Feet first, my toe stretches toward the plate. A slightly raised edge of home plate catches my shoe. I am safe, but my body is hurled forward and my foot does not follow. The loud crack of my anklebone is heard by the catcher and the umpire.

Today, instead of playing second base, I am in the second bed of room 232 recuperating from surgery to repair my ankle. I tell the twenty-year-old patient in bed one, "Just goes to show you, you can't count your chickens until they hatch. I thought I was headed toward state competition and I didn't make it to the first game."

She looks at me and sneers. "Aren't you too old to be playing games?"

"Too old?"

"Yes, too old."

"No. Aren't you too young to be having a nervous breakdown?"

ANDRE DE KORVIN

Leaving The Village

My village sorcerer said: "There the lights of temples stand on the edge of asphalt lakes and the dream tiger is extinct in the shifting desert of graveyard shifts. Old metaphors are left to rot in the market place." I still left for the city. At highspeed, tree tops paint a green dawn on the curved canvas of gray horizons and foliage, flowers closed, dreams at dusk of nostalgia on winter's white pages. Train roared sorrow to downcast trees and the sun spun, gold record playing over and over, man is alone. (Flaming notes drift over the world, now and then scientists catch them in telescopes, giving them names of ancient gods.) And the conductor, a little hard of hearing, said: "They're playing one way ticket on the heartbreak express." In the city, clock towers always point their hands at time: inept policemen trying to arrest a runaway child. I remember, the consensus of noon chimes was "Guilty." Unstable years deported to daydreaming, display their signs on the curb. Daydreaming . . . . No trees stood on the playground. It was so cold, tears could have created perpetual motion bouncing on the asphalt, a metronome marking the rhythm of sorrow. I never forgot the great slide hiding half of the sky. My village tumbling into bottomless years.

ANDRE DE KORVIN

Texas Dreaming

The giant mirror starts to spin. People come from all parts of the world to read the messages flashing across the dazzling surface, everyone hoping to catch a glimpse of themselves in the glass. "Tom," flashes the mirror. "Tom, there's no seismic drift." "Tom," a billion people whisper, "Tom, there's no seismic drift." The mirror expands. It is now impossible to see its outer edges. At times, images seem distorted. Maps of Alabama, Louisiana and Texas drift across the glass. A gas station attendant appears in the middle of the glass. "Prices are down!" he shouts and his image shrinks, lost somewhere in the middle of Texas. A temple drifts into the empty space. A starry-eyed man tells the world, "The lights of temples shine on the edge of cement waters and the dream tiger walks no longer in the forest of derricks." "The dream tiger," a billion people sigh. "The dream tiger is almost extinct." A lake floods a large part of the mirror. A sign proclaims, "Dangerous currents, this is the heart of Texas." "Ah Texas," a billion people chant, "this is the heart of Texas." The starry-eyed man pulls a throbbing heart from his attaché case. The heart leaves his hand, ascends quickly becoming a dot. "Look at the rose of Texas," a billion people scream. "Andres," flashes the mirror. "Andres, you made an error. The lone star is not anchored to your balcony. Look within for the lone star." When I wake, the man with the attaché case is by my side. I want to tell him the dream tiger still walks. My heart beats faster. A small star rises over the blue valley of my lips.

PAULINE M. DELANEY

Crime Stoppers

Josie McDaniel, brandishing a tire wrench with the price tag
still flapping, bursts out of the Highway Stop & Shop as I'm
pulling onto the driveway.

"Thief," she yells. "Stop that thief!"

I roll down my patrol car window. "Having trouble,
Honey?" I ask.

"Trouble! Do you call robbery trouble?" She shifts her
tobacco wad from one cheek to the other and strides to my
car. "You saw that red Ferrari that just took off? The driver
stole seven dollars!"

"Seven whole dollars?"

"Wipe that silly grin off your face, Mr. Deputy Sheriff,"
she says. "Robbery—no matter how much—is a crime. I want
it stopped." She leans in my car window. "Radio the sheriff."

I flip on my two-way and start listing Josie's complaints.
"Red Ferrari, kid driver, filled his tank with Supreme, came
inside; to pay, Josie thought. Instead he goes to her john."

"Right so far," says Josie, turning her head to spit.

I lower my voice. "Chief," I say, "you know how Josie
is about her 'ladies-only' john; she makes men use the
outhouse."

Wiping away tobacco juice, Josie turns back to me: "The
kid comes out, grabs a four-ninety-five Hershey bar, peels
off the wrapper and flings down a five. Then he says, 'Keep
the change'! A nickel tip! For me! I own the place! I tell him
what I think of him and his tip. He backs out the door, jumps
in the car, takes off. And then I realize he hasn't paid for his
gas!"

"Maybe he paid at the pump?"

"Him? Ha!" She grabs my mike, flings it to the seat.
"What do you think you're paid for? Get moving."

70

Before Josie has time to decide she's mad at me instead of the Ferrari driver, I take off. The red car is stopped at the traffic light this side of town. Switching on my roof lights, I hit the siren. The Ferrari goes from zero to ninety in less time than it takes me to blink. Knowing I'm out-classed, I radio the town cops, and continue on to watch the fun.

The Ferrari zooms through town like a NASA rocket. Mattie Lou Moffatt runs her pink Cadillac halfway through the jewelry store window getting out of its way. A pickup, dodging Mrs. Moffatt, skims so close to Jim Hamilton's retriever, the dog thinks he's hit, yelps and runs. Jim storms out of the sporting goods store, yanks out his gun, aims at the pickup. He misses, but the driver jumps the curb, knocking over the town's re-cycling barrel and scattering a year's collection of glass and scrap metal.

Dodging litter, I take a short cut, come out at the city limits sign. This sign also marks the line between us and Highland County.

Just across that line is Highland County's own Sheriff Wilcox. Hands on his hips, he's grinning that smug grin he gets when he horns in on our crime. A sawhorse is planted in the middle of the highway.

The Ferrari screeches around a corner. Wilcox raises one hand, steps onto the pavement. The car shoots past him and his sawhorse, slices across a curve, disappears over a hill.

Moments later I hear tires squeal, then fence posts splintering, then . . . nothing. I speed past Wilcox as he runs for his car.

Just over the crest of the hill is the Ferrari, nose-first in a gully. Slamming on my brakes, I jump out, run to check the driver. Wilcox, gun drawn, is right behind me.

A kid with a bloody nose and a knot on his head the size of a Texas grapefruit is buckled in the Ferrari's front seat. His arms shoot up.

"Driver's license," growls the sheriff. The kid fumbles, produces a college ID and the title to the car. Wilcox glares at

71

the papers, flings them back. "I said, 'driver's license'."

The kid fumbles again, finally hands a rumpled fold to the sheriff.

Wilcox's face turns the color of cooked beets. "Expired! Outta that car! You're under arrest."

Hands trembling, the kid unfastens the seat belt, steps from the car. Wilcox grabs him, whirls him around, snaps on handcuffs. Gun at the kid's back, he marches him to his patrol car, shoves him into the back seat, jumps in front and roars off for the Highland County jail.

I ring Josie on my cell phone and tell her the good news. I hear silence. Finally Josie sighs. "I found my seven dollars. On a pile of newspapers by the cash register. I guess you better radio Wilcox to turn the kid loose."

Then—I can almost hear her brain shift gears—Josie says, "No! Lock him up! He shoulda asked before he used my john."

WENDY DIMMETT

The Garden

I think I know how God feels, being outside things. Yet, he had to be to sculpt us, give us a name, and set us in motion. On that last day in Paradise, he washed his hands until the Sabbath was over and alarm clocks rang all the way into Monday. After that, in all his omnipotence, He simply watched: Holy Spectator, Divine Critic. Out of love, I arranged the beauty of a garden and I marveled at the perfection of my creation. I still do. You can't imagine how green the shadows of my trees are or how still the heart of rocks in my garden. The dirt remembers me, prophesies all summer with golden dandelions who grow grey hair and leave on the wind's temptation. The sun is my wisdom. The grass makes me real. Everything is my wish until the birds I love drop like warnings on butterflies I would save—if I could. But here, my creation takes on a life of its own. Time multiplies. I close the gate and think how right it is that I am the only thing out of place here.

WENDY DIMMETTE

A Bridge Player's Journal

I never had time for computers because I have this mad
passion for card games. If I didn't belong to my bridge club,
I'd open a speak-easy, some run-down place with a red door
where regulars knock three times: Once loud, once soft, then
loud again, where gamblers hide their cards and I rake money
into a hat (along with an ace or two) just before the police
spill through the door shouting This is a Raid! I'd play my
aces then, offer them a chance to win. They can't. So they
leave without even a goodbye. My dream . . . until that accident
coming home from the bridge tournament we lost. I had
enough broken bones to keep me down two months. The gang
met anyway. And I knew they were talking about me, how
reckless I can be, how I take chances. I don't care what they
say, losing that tournament was not my fault. But it depressed
me and I took more pain pills that made me use uninhibited
language about their abilities, too. I was already mad when
my son suggested computer lessons. I'm a card Shark, I
screamed, not a blasted engineer! He shrugged, said computers
are easy as shuffling or dealing. He plugged it in, turned on
the magic. We'll play Solitaire, he said, and the memory of
my pessimistic Bridge Buddies began to fade. I smiled at my
dear son and said sweetly, You can go now. I don't want any
more lessons. He grinned like a kid and closed the door. He'll
be back. And I'm glad. I want to show him how good I am at
this Solitaire thing. I can beat the machine with two broken
arms. And that just shows to go you when a cat is holding a
mouse, you never know what a deuce can do.

74

JAMES O. DOBBS

Some Final Thoughts

Mullets. Big-eyed, gaping mullets, gulping in air I will soon no longer breathe. Sitting on the other side of the glass to witness this, a legal requirement, but they aren't really concerned with the law, they are curious, thrill-seeking warps enchanted by death. My death. If I lifted my head from this gurney and gave them a big toothy smile, half of them would faint, and the other half would wet their pants. I wish I could curse them with blindness. I don't want them to see me tremble.

What can I think about in the next few minutes that will allow me to endure this without screaming? I can't think about what they are doing with their straps and tubes. They are like shaved Egyptian priests wrapping a mummy, slow, careful to place each winding strip just so in woven linen perfection. Some of them are enjoying it; sadists having a little mental orgasm as they bring me to the omega point. Solemn hypocrites, rubber-gloved killers. Maybe I can just go blank. How can I do that?

A little sting. Not bad. A warmth floods me. What the hell is this? Wait a minute! I see her fright-wide eyes, her moving lips. I crush them with my savage kiss. I crush her body with my thrusting anger. I despise her innocence, her virginity, her privilege. I feel her slim throat pulsing in my tightening hands. I smash my blood-red rage against the concrete floor, again and again, hating what I can never be and never have.

My final breaths are sucked out of seven years of stubborn silence, hopeless appeals, cynicism. And I die, reliving for all eternity the act that has taken two lives: hers and mine.

House of Mirrors

The first day Richard joined the law firm, Marissa noticed how outgoing, handsome, and well built he was, unlike all the other stodgy men in her office. Initially, even the gold wedding band on his finger didn't seem to concern her. It was the one on her finger that gave her a guilty conscience.

Marissa's eight year marriage to Mark had somehow become trite and predictable—conversation between them was sparse, and weekends were mostly spent taking care of household tasks, with the exception of an occasional night out. Worst of all, their romantic interludes seemed dutiful and were practically scheduled.

As Richard and Marissa's caseload escalated, they found themselves spending more time at the office after hours. Their late evenings increasingly became spiced with flirtation and subtle innuendoes.

"You seem to be the type to have a weakness for white-chocolate covered strawberries," said Richard as he handed Marissa a small box containing the delectable treat. "Indulge yourself," he said as he looked intently into her eyes. He was close enough to kiss her when his secretary walked in with documents needing his signature.

Marissa found Richard enticing. She knew the emotions brewing between the two were a step away from becoming . . . improper.

Then came the call. It was Richard's wife inviting Marissa and her husband to a dinner party at their house.

"I'm looking forward to meeting you," said Marissa as she tried to picture her over the telephone. "Can I bring anything?"

"How about a dessert?" the wife said in a genial tone.

That entire week Marissa kept thinking what it was going to be like to sit across the dinner table from Richard's wife, knowing how intense and inappropriate her feelings were for him.

As Marissa got into the car with her husband, she wondered why she ever accepted the dinner invitation. She wished she had declined the offer from the beginning, but it was too late.

As they got out of the car, Marissa thought how well the stately two-story house seemed to fit Richard. The landscaped yard was incredible. It could have easily been featured in a home and garden magazine. The *Yard of the Month* sign in front of his house validated her opinion.

The woman who shared Richard's bed stood at the door. She didn't fit the image Marissa had conjured in her mind. Richard's wife was simple and rather plain looking. For some strange reason, Marissa liked her instantly. Under different circumstances they could have become best friends.

The interior of the house was as impressive as the outside, except a little more revealing. The mantle displayed the family portrait: Richard, his wife and their beautiful nine-year-old twin daughters. Yet the man in the picture looked nothing like the suave Richard from the office. He even seemed to walk differently in his house—with a lot less strut and confidence.

At work he was as titillating as a Jaguar on the highway. At home, his wife said he enjoyed watching "Three Stooges" reruns, and the programs on PBS. Later that evening, pictures revealed that Richard's ideal vacation consisted of seven days of peace and quiet on his family farm in the hill country.

Even Mark wasn't that dull—he liked going to the movies, dancing, vacationing in the tropics, and was known to come home with a racy video every now and then. Of course, that was before they grew too comfortable in the marriage. By mid-evening, Mark seemed to be gaining appeal.

As conversation went back and forth in the living room, Marissa sipped on a glass of wine, occasionally glancing at Richard. She expected to see a glimmer of that seductive smile that tended to leave her breathless. Yet his smile now seemed ordinary . . . as his spouse, and his life. Marissa didn't know whether it was the Chardonnay that impeded her from seeing the flirtatious Richard, so she declined the third glass, hoping to find a trace of the man she had desired for the last few weeks.

After dinner Richard managed to steal a moment alone with Marissa out on the patio. Suddenly, slick Richard was back.

"Ready for a slice of that strawberry pie?" he asked as he leaned in to kiss her.

"As tempting as it is, I think I'll pass," she said as she pulled away. "It's probably not as good as it looks."

JOYCE M. FISCHER

Communion

I am an old woman and she is my second child to die.

When the nurse turns the machines off and leaves the room, I give thanks for this child's middle-aged body, for the loves she had, the places she went. I bring her ring finger to my lips, bite the nail smooth with my front teeth the way I used to when even the baby scissors seemed dangerous next to her newborn fingers.

My first child died in fireworks seen 'round the world. Twenty cameras trained on my face as we counted down, clapped at the rocket's launch. Then our hands stopped moving and dropped to our sides as the long, white tube exploded, twisting a graceful curve downward, trailing the most beautiful sparks.

Only one news team had the nerve to keep the camera rolling. Many thought the anguish on my face obscene, cursed them for holding in history what should have been offered up to heaven.

But there are no pictures of me minutes later, hidden around the side of the grandstand, my face upturned, hoping to catch a bit of ash like a snowflake on my tongue in the hot Florida sun.

JOYCE M. FISCHER

Studebaker

I sat behind you for thousands of miles as you drove us away from yet another life into a new new one still fresh with the ignorance of your mistakes. No one burned bridges better than you. Their blackened remains were your greatest success.

I blazed my eyes into your flesh, imagined your screams of pain as you burned. I didn't want to think of the new classroom, always the last seat in the last row, the three too-short dresses alternated until kids caught on and started to laugh, the teacher overly kind. Then it was weeks or sometimes months before the late-night calls, bill collectors standing on a porch or stoop, refusing to leave until they were paid.

My sore heart believed sometimes that if I just stared hard enough, a vessel in your brain would burst like fireworks, your hands would trail down from the big steering wheel of the rusting Studebaker and the car would lay down sideways in a wide ditch, your body quite dead as I climbed out the backseat window. I would emerge, wipe my hands on my pedal pushers, walk down the empty road into whatever life I chose, out of sight before the wheels even stopped spinning.

Now that your neck is creased and bent, white hair sparse upon it, I am left with a nine-year-old's rage, knotted in my body like turpentine rags, waiting for a spark.

JOYCE M. FISCHER

Cistercian Day

3:30 a.m. Remember: Desire

He is stiff and troubled as the bell rings for first office, his breath not his breath but the breath of each other monk in the large sleeping room. In council, he celebrates his decision to come to fraternal life after forty, truly choosing God after a full knowledge of the greater world, unlike some fair-cheeked brothers who took vows at nineteen. But his dreams call sometimes with an ungodly force, and the morning bell brings him back from long kisses in a Taipei bar with a Japanese sailor whose skin feels like the well-washed softness of his grandmother's dishtowels.

5:30 a.m. Reflect: Silence

A world without speech is not a world of silence. It is a world of intricate knowing, of sharing one body, one mind. He can tell by the click of the spoon on the bowl that Brother Benedict is feeling contemplative. Brother Marcus shows his weariness in his soft sigh as he lays down his napkin. True silence is only met alone in the chapel, one candle burning, yet the beat of his own heart follows him there.

6:30 a.m. Rejoice: Sunrise

He folds his hands together on his lap and feels perfection. The sun creeps above the first blue hill, glancing off the surface of the Shenandoah, spilling magnificence onto his rough wool socks and sandals. In simple moments like this, he can be God.

12:30 p.m. Renounce: Bread

Usually life with nothing is easy, amazingly so. But sometimes the sight of the trucks full of bread, pulling out to

81

distribute hundreds of loaves at $2.89 each, touched by a monk's hand, fill him with the sin of pride. It was he who had the thought one day, "this is my body, broken for you. . . ." It had been he who had first believed that they could support the monastery with something as simple as bread, as simple as faith.

7:30 p.m. Retreat: Sunset

Their valley lies in shadow first, the sun below the mountain long before it leaves this part of the earth. After final office there is only an hour before sleep, a precious slice of time that finds him always there, standing on the back pasture hill, his brothers' chants still soft in his ears. The sky fades from crimson to salmon to periwinkle to the deepest blue. Gold flecks turn to silver, and then to white. He looks down the far pasture across the river to the simple line of white crosses nestled against the base of the mountain.

Unblocked

Laura looked away from the half-filled computer screen with its impatient blinking cursor, to glance at the television. There, several elegantly clad men and women were crowded around a body.

She picked up the phone and punched a number. "Hi, it's me. What on earth is going on? No, I haven't been watching that close. I'm on the computer. Have you read anything about that guy leaving the show?"

A finger poked her shoulder. Laura jerked in surprise, then turned to see her husband's angry face.

"I'll call you back."

She put down the phone and gave him her best smile. "Hi, honey, what are you doing home?"

"I have to go to Dallas for a few days. But that's not the problem." He threw a large stack of envelopes on her desk. "It's lucky I happened to stop and check the box. At least two weeks' mail. You've missed the mortgage payment again."

She quailed at his discovery, then gave a surreptitious peek at the beckoning blink of the cursor.

He grabbed beneath her chin and yanked her to face him. "Can't you pay attention to anything but that computer? It's almost two-thirty. The breakfast dishes are still on the table and I'll bet you the bed hasn't been made."

He stomped into the bedroom with Laura close behind. "Just as I suspected. Instead of doing what you're supposed to, you sit at that damn computer all day with the television blaring!"

Laura bridled. "I'm trying to write. The tube's on for the noise. You know I can't stand the ringing in my ears."

"Face it, Laura, you're not a writer, and you never will be. Why don't you do something useful for a change? Get a job, volunteer, wash the dishes, make the bed."

"I'm blocked," she wailed. "The words are there, but they just won't come."

Her husband grunted, then stomped into his closet where he yanked down two suits and grabbed several white shirts.

"Why are you so angry? You've been so angry, lately."

He threw the clothes on the unmade bed. "Wouldn't you be angry if you came home to a pig sty every day? Had a wife who doesn't pick up the mail or pay the bills? Look at yourself. I haven't seen you in anything but that ratty warm-up outfit for weeks."

Laura cringed. "I was going to clean up before you got home."

"Oh, sure you were. The house is filthy. You're a slob. And all you can talk about is being blocked. Where's my fold-over?"

"In the basement. I'll get it." Laura turned to go downstairs, her stomach churning. She hated negotiating the narrow steps cascading over thirty feet to the cement floor below. The house, which sat on a small bluff overlooking a lake, was originally designed with three floors and a basement. To save money, her husband had the architect cut what was to be the children's floor, creating the treacherous descent.

"No. That's my bailiwick. I know where everything is." He pushed her aside and headed down the back stairs to the kitchen with Laura at his heels.

She surveyed the shambles of her kitchen. It was true. She had abandoned her husband for the writing life: long wonderful days filled with new people and exotic places. People and places she created. Days that often ended seated across the dinner table from an angry, demanding man. What happened? Where did that fun-loving person she married go? Was it when they found they couldn't have children? It wasn't her fault. He forgot to tell her about the raging case of mumps his freshman year.

Her husband flung open the cellar door with such force that it ricocheted, momentarily knocking him off balance.

Laura gasped and clutched for his sleeve. "Oh, darling,

please be careful."

He shook her hand away. "Don't be such a weenie."

"I was afraid you might fall. Those steps are so steep."

He turned. The look on his face was pure hate. "That was the plan. To keep you out."

When her husband turned away, the answer came. So simple—so perfect.

She shoved as hard as she could, pitching him over the low railing into the darkness.

"Oh?" That was all he said before the thud.

Laura listened for a moment, shut and locked the door and made her way up the stairs to the telephone beside her computer.

"Hi, it's me again. Sorry for the interruption. Oh, my gosh, that guy's in the morgue and that toothy woman's kissing him goodbye. I guess they're definitely writing him out of the story. What a shame, he was so good."

KAREN GERHARDT

Coyote Night

Almost every weekend we drive out to one of the ranch roads just before dusk. We park on the shoulder of a gravel road, turn off the engine, and wait . . . watch . . . listen . . . for whatever the evening brings.

Ten years ago, or maybe it was fifteen, he heard the crying of coyotes off in the distance. He's never heard them since. But he keeps a covenant with the land, a hope that nature prevails, no matter how deeply man scars its perfection.

I have no such covenant, but I've seen a paisano dance in the road and a diamondback rattler glide through the sand. Once, a mother quail marched her brood across the road like a sergeant herding raw recruits. And a pair of deer melted into the brush . . . still as fenceposts . . . exposed by the glistening whites of their eyes.

Far from the noise and the lights of town, we breathe in unison with the heartbeat of the planet. Feel the warm mantle of Mother Earth. Revive.

One night before Christmas, after I had endured an unplanned hospital stay, he held my pain-swollen hand in his and drove out of town without asking where, or even if, I wanted to go. He knew.

The prevailing southeast wind buffeted prickly pear pads and tunas. Whirled through clumps of buffalo grass and rabbit brush. Rattled drying bean pods on ashen mesquite limbs. Crickets and insects whistled and chirped, clattered and clicked, murmured and hummed a pulsating chorus, the chant of the earth.

The silent night is very loud, indeed.

We parked on the side of the gravel road and watched the moon rise high above a distant tree line. Hang suspended in the velvet sky, bright as a strobe, casting opalescent shadows across cactus-mottled grassland, slipping past fence lines to shed silver stardust on red corduroy fields.

Then, above the noisy stillness of the night, we heard high-pitched yipping from the direction of the tree line. We sat forward, every molecule alert, straining to listen. The yipping came again, like an echo this time. Not the bark or howl of a dog, but the distinct, eager cry of the coyote. Several of them. Moving through the safety of the brush.

He clutched my hand. I sucked in my breath . . . remembered the pain of needle pricks . . . sharp-pointed canines plunging deep into veins.

The yipping came closer.

Liquid shadows, they crossed the gravel road and kept moving south.

We watched and listened, not daring to speak.

Like seasons, they vanished.

We returned to paved streets and palm trees, bright lights and bursting noise . . . the barbed wire and fenceposts of domesticated lives. But the delight of discovery pulsed between us . . . nature's frontier held fast to its ancestral home, keeping the covenant.

Somewhere between the ranch road and the courthouse square, the pain vanished into the shadowy underbrush of the past . . . moving south.

J. LEE GOODMAN

Hourglass

The crystal hourglass seemed to glare at me as I waited impatiently. The sand had run its course through the pinched middle, and a whimsical pointed dune lay at the bottom. Streams of sunlight dancing across the amber grains made them glitter like diamonds. I stared transfixed at the conical dune. Its perfect shape had grown from a steady stream of plummeting grit, each grain contributing to its maturity. Closing my eyes, I could picture the initial grains bouncing aimlessly around the bottom, only to be forced into a foundation as gravity pulled more sand through the narrow aperture. The emerging cone was beautiful, a new bud—fresh and undisturbed. The flower of time bloomed as the last grains crowned, majestically, the conical dune. A nurse touched my shoulder. "It's time to remove the bandages," she said. I nervously rose from my reverie, and my arm brushed the hourglass. It shattered when it hit the floor. The whimsy was gone.

For Linda, who died of breast cancer at 42

NANCY GUSTAFSON

Memory of an Orange

She shivered through the war years, saw her parents shot, neighbors and friends hauled away in trucks; said she huddled in a gray alley, never shed a tear in all those years. The day a GI in a speeding jeep tossed her half an orange, she leaped, caught it like a fly at third base, held it dripping in her hand, inhaled its pungent fragrance, devoured the tangy peel and membranes, its sweet sections bursting in her mouth, licked her lips, unwilling to waste a precious drop of this gift—more than a gift: a covenant with life, like sacred host on her tongue. She buried her face in her hands until the scent disappeared like a golden sunset behind dark mountains. When only the memory of the orange remained, she sobbed.

NANCY GUSTAFSON

Immaculate Music

Steeped in candlelight and incense, I kneel to ponder the mysteries of the Passion. Priest, lector, and altar servers stand in the vestibule, ready for the processional. Mrs. Mary Agnes Montague, church pianist for forty years, enters the sanctuary through a side door. She is dressed in her best pink suit; rhinestone pin and matching earrings are winking fireflies. Her head, cupped by white hair like a starched lace doily, blazes a path to the crucifix; she bows reverently, then shuffles to the piano. Mary Agnes Montague rests a peaceful gaze upon her audience, signaling the mass is about to begin.

Encumbered by knotted knuckles she rustles through the hymnal, finds the entrance anthem: Page 73—"Immaculate Mary," a favorite. Her hands, poised above the ivory keys, are beautifully manicured; a gold wedding band on her left hand, a grandmother's ring with fifteen colored stones on her right. These hands tripped lightly over ivory keys a few years ago, seldom slipping. But today, arthritic fingers fumble around before they strike the first chord. The sanctuary fills with brave voices accompanied by the piano and the click clicking of pink polymer nails. Rare souls with perfect pitch cringe at occasional discord.

Mass ends with a stately procession to the front door, while Mrs. Montague stands victorious by her piano, waiting for the few people who will thank her for her music. The light of her sweet face beams into mine as she grasps my hands in her own. She smiles with her whole face: skin a translucent moiré, newly-minted white teeth and brown eyes, nearly hidden by heavy lids—an icon more beautiful than a Botticelli Madonna. In a crackled whisper, she tells me a bit of news about a mutual acquaintance and asks about my children. Is my daughter coming home for Christmas? How is my son doing since his divorce? How are the grandchildren? I will come again and again to ponder the mysteries of her passion and the immaculate music of her life.

ALBERT HALEY

Aurora

Tonight the skies are torn by the white, green, red ghostly expansion and contraction; a world of phenomena, arcing into the northern belt where the earth forty days ago caved into snow and ice-blast. Tonight, this deep December night, the white-coated creatures that hoof and creep and paw across the plain receive a hint of how their world will end: fevered heat, spun out by celestial, whirling, rayed wheels. More amazed than thankful, the land life risks everything, emerging from mounds and dens in the woods, attracted by the impossible presence of flickering midnight shadows and a sticky sound in the lower atmosphere like the rustling of taffeta. And now coming behind them are the thin-boned people whose eyes crave relief from the day-night darkness of winter. These last northern inhabitants stare upwards at electric current sheets flowing into gases, a masterpiece of potentiality and magnetic collision dispatched by the sun. But the sight cannot be verbally embraced by those known as frequent mouthers of words because it lives by its own breath and inhales starlight and blows it out again from the west to the east; the patterns changing and evolving, intensifying and fading, the labor of eons occurring in one crackling minute. Just drifting, floating, falling; great, inviolable radiating light making distant mountaintops that are thick with snow reflect the atomic vitality pumped through veins of space; now sailing upwards majestically, more focused and shimmering still; until eyes and minds will go no farther; and all of land life is left behind, feeling wing-stripped by the pale and bright wand waving of heaven. Tonight this must be the sign, the last sign, sufficient to send the powerless, the two-footed, the brain heavy to bed and new dreams of fire consuming fire.

ALBERT HALEY

The Unknown Planet

At the edge of our universe lies the unknown planet. It is the coldest orb of all. It hangs without pulse, shadow, or radiowave tremble. Silent, undetectable but steadily tracking. And as the rockets fire and the silver tube descends, casting the first light that has ever flickered over its slight immensity, the unknown planet does not sigh or worry. It remains Pharaoh-like in a tomb of its own, bound in dusty immobility, no curator's labels attached. A plain survey of its surface will reveal it to be solid black, dimpled, waffled and grooved, the victim of some hard iron feudal age of the cosmos or perhaps the torture device itself, barbed and annular and skull smashing. The spacemen's feet make no impression upon it. Their curiosity and enthusiasm cannot bait the unknown planet in its impervious, blind, stone confident trajectory and hiddenness. Like love never begun, or hatred concealed, the dark ball remains behind the other, grander universal pretensions (how do you explain fat gas Jupiter? ring drunk Saturn?). Could one call it mystery? When the explorers leave in a blaze of hydrogen they carry with them less than a micro-speck of samples of what is too durable to chip. A dull, tool-defying conundrum stowed in plastic crates. In the end, no name can be given this thing that is out there, has been out there, will always be so *far, far,* out there, magnificent and indifferent, upon which all knowledge must stumble at the edge. Didn't we suspect? Like Pluto we should have theorized its presence long before we made the necessary journey to glimpse, touch, turn away. Even now we are forgetting. But it is there. It is. It. I.

JOYCE POUNDS HARDY

Homecoming

We didn't have a soldier coming home; not one that we could call by name or one that we had ached to hold again. But we were there, drawn by some need to share that victory, that safe return, to show our pride, if only with our little flags and smiles. The troops arrived, erupted from their trucks, then reassembled briefly. And we, caught up in patriotic fervor, feeling every cadence in our hearts, fell into line and marched beside them through the hangar doors and ran like family, rejoicing as if they belonged to us—to all of us, who'd watched each hour, day by day, in living color, hurting, praying, wishing there had been some other way for peace and freedom than a war. We stood there crying with those strangers, turning toward reunions like sunflowers turning with the sun, sharing their warmth, reflecting their joy, holding our children's hands and knowing they would never forget this moment—just as I have never forgotten such love, the feel of my father's strong arms in his starched khaki shirt, the clean soap smell of him as he lifted me high over his head and said it was good to be home.

Ft. Hood, Sunday, April 14, 1991
Desert Storm

Sound Bites

The KLUNK in the backyard shot a ripple of reactions through my head. Years, eons it seems, of reacting the same way to sounds coming through the drawn curtains, sounds somewhere off in the night: a dog, a cat, a squirrel, a raccoon, an intruder, all possibles. But my reaction was predictable, a well-honed rational habit—check to see it the garage door were down. I never could remember if I had shut it even though most of the time I had. Trouble is now there is no garage door to put down, in fact, there is no garage—bulldozed months ago—gone, missing-in-action, kaput! However, that did not keep me from needing to close it. Nor did it keep me from heading toward it ten times a day to get a bucket or a shovel or a screwdriver. Habit can be a nuisance, and this one is sad. It's embarrassing to bound out the back door to get the car out of the garage only to remember it's in the street. I never thought I'd miss going out there to do the washing—hot or cold, mosquitos or mice, rain or shine—but I do. The laundromat sucks. It's Spring and I am lost—no shelves of clay pots, potting soil, ant spray, mosquito spray, people spray, and gardening tools, fertilizer and old paint cans, empty bubble gum cartons by the hundreds, driftwood collected on our beloved deer lease, thirty years worth of holey rocks (the envy of every grandmother on the block who builds forts and castles with her grandchildren,) Coleman lanterns and stoves, fans, temporary fencing for my granddogs. Daddy's ancient tools that had been my childhood treasures, cots for company, picnic tables for oversized crowds, twenty-six folding chairs for Christmas dinner, a spinnaker pole whose sailboat was long sold, snow skis that had never seen snow, a clown's head sprinkler, a blow-up backyard pool, a slip and slide, lawn chairs, floats, crab nets, minnow strainers, bait buckets, rope, string, wire, (we were never without wire because Daddy said never be without wire!) baseball bats—peewee to college, tennis balls, basketballs, a pogo stick, mops, dowels, a driftwood cross with Christmas lights on it that lit up when the garage door went up, a grinder, a vice, a zillion rusty nails and screws, a rusty saw (precious still because Lynn had bought it for her daddy when it was bigger than she was,) a heavy duty army chest that had lived half its life in the back of our old pickup filled to the brim with tarps, jackups, cables, gloves, flash lights, tow chains, tire chains, work towels, and of course, hunting gear. Even the barbeque grill with a dozen never-used attachments was gone. All gone, hopefully to be reassembled in a far better place if I live long enough to see the new garage finished. But, like the amputee who constantly feels his lost leg itching and needing a good scratch, I jump to check on the KLUNK, forgetting for the hundredth time that there's nothing out there—nothing but a lifetime of memories.

JOYCE HARLOW

Trials and Tribulations

The trials were hard enough to bear, but then the tribulations set in. When brother run off with that floozy back in Happy Hollow, she had to live through every gory detail with Effie Mae. And then if that didn't beat all, the preacher up and declared he was moving back to Milwaukee to live with another man. Worst of all was that gall dern twister ripping up the apple orchard and blowing the outhouse away. Now she had to go behind the bushes and there was no apple jelly to go on her breakfast biscuit.

But then the tribulations were another sort altogether. Franklin had been gone nigh onto a year. He'd left home before, but he always managed to find his way back. She had lived through the first Thanksgiving alone with her daughter's cooking and her son-in-law's family clucking over her misfortune. She broke away as soon as it was passable, vowing never to go through that again.

And now Christmas was just around the corner. She had refused all invitations to celebrate at someone else's house, preferring instead to be alone.

From the attic she pulled down musty boxes labeled "Christmas" and stacked them in the parlor. Inside yellowed tissue had come loose from the tree ornaments, and she shook mouse droppings from its contents.

She bent back the mangled points of an aluminum foil star. Billie Bob had made it when he was in the first grade. She combed her fingers through the tangled tinsel taped on each point and pictured her grown son in that jail cell over in Big Reedy. He never could handle his liquor and the sheriff was plum fed up and had vowed to keep him through the holidays. Thank goodness there were no babies to miss the daddy that could only shoot blanks.

96

But those five kids of her daughter made up for the empty nest of her son. She had a list a mile long of what each one wanted for Christmas. Apparently her daughter had never taught them its true meaning.

Now where was that manger set that she had bought last year at the dime store over in Brownsville? She riffled through the rest of the boxes and there it was in the bottom of the last one. She pulled out a plaster Mary, Joseph and Christ Child. She glanced around the room and decided the windowsill would be a good place for it.

Franklin liked to sit in the rocking chair and soak up the sun that climbed across the frosty panes. She guessed it wouldn't be any use to hang up his stocking.

A peck at the door and in rushed her daughter. She had two jars of apple jelly tied up with big red bows. Seeing as how she knew her mother missed the sweets, she had just run in for a minute. Seems she was on her way to work on the long list her children had wrote out for Santa. And then she was gone just like the whirlwind that dashed dried leaves and pine needles into the corners of her porch.

The whistling kettle reminded her that it was time for an afternoon respite. Before she could pour the tea, the door banged open and Billie Bob sauntered into the room stomping snow onto her good rag rug. He told her as how the sheriff let him out for the holidays, but he had to promise to turn himself in after New Year's.

And Lord have mercy, her son pulled out a yellow striped bundle of fur from his jacket. It was Franklin. And that tomcat had a big red bow around his neck to boot.

Peers like it was going to be a good Christmas after all.

97

LINDA J. HELMAN

Second Best

"**W**hatsa matter with you? Why don't you use the green cleanser? Your sister always used the green stuff. Cleaned my bathroom every morning; kept it sparkling. If you cared about your mother, you'd use the green cleanser."

Claudia cringed and counted to ten. "I'll buy some—tomorrow." It was her turn to care for her mother and she couldn't talk back to her. She wasn't raised that way.

After Claudia's sister Angela passed away, their mother had to move in with Claudia. A tough situation for both of them. They hadn't gotten along as far back as Claudia could remember. Angela had been the favorite. Claudia was sure their lives would be hell as her mother hadn't said a nice word to her for years.

Her mother was a feisty ninety-two with a sharp tongue and a cane to match. She'd whack the furniture or the back of Claudia's legs to get attention, whichever was closer. George, Claudia's cat, had taken refuge in the bedroom, refusing to go near the older woman after she smacked him with the cane for trying to wrap around her legs. Claudia wasn't pleased, but held her tongue through a sense of duty. Besides, it would only have led to another argument.

Over several generations, the families held onto the belief that the youngest daughter was responsible for the care of the mother. Angela had complained of being a prisoner in her own home. As was the custom, she never married but devoted her life to her mother. With Angela gone from a sudden heart attack, the duty fell to Claudia. And, if her mother managed to send Claudia to her grave, then Maria would have a shot. Claudia was a widow, and for once in her life, was pleased Al wasn't around. She was sure he'd be another target of abuse and equally sure he wouldn't have stayed quiet about it.

"Good." Her mother continued. "And change the sheets. Your stupid cat jumped on my bed."

Claudia knew the cat would not go anywhere near the woman or her bed, but she didn't say anything. Pulling out a fresh set of bedding, she changed the sheets and took them to the laundry room.

Her mother trailed after her. "I hope you're not planning on making that crap again for dinner. A person could die with the stuff you serve."

"What stuff, Ma?"

"You know. That mess you call lasagna. Your sister could make a better lasagna with her eyes closed. She used fresh ingredients. Had a little garden in the back, grew her own tomatoes. Made the pasta with that little machine. She didn't waste her money buying junk at the store and passing it off as real food to her poor mother. She cared about what I ate."

Life continued this way between mother and daughter until two years later. Claudia's mother became infirm and the doctor suggested a nursing home. Claudia quickly agreed. It would give her a chance to get her life back together. Take the burden off her shoulders.

The ambulance came to transport her mother. Claudia watched as the men placed the older woman on a stretcher. "I hope you enjoy your new home, Ma. I'll come and see you soon."

The old woman focused on the attendants. "Whatsa matter with you? Can't you take it easy? I'm an old lady. Watch out for the doorway. Where's my cane? I ain't going nowhere without my cane."

A week passed and Claudia hadn't spoken to her mother. But she found herself buying green cleanser and she had planted a garden. The quiet in the house disturbed her and accentuated the empty spot in her heart. There was only one thing to do. She grabbed her car keys.

DOROTHY HERRON

The Automobile Club

An urgent conversation with my mother. Asking me to come spend the night. Leave my children sleeping and go to AA meetings with my father. Why? Because she is exhausted. She can't go to meetings with him every night of the week and still get up and go to work in the morning.

Why does Daddy have to go to Auto Club meetings every night of the week? I ask, incredulous

Followed by the stunning accusation—Sarah Sue, your father is an alcoholic!

She fairly screams at me, then recovers her well modulated voice. But I can't hear what she says because her perfectly manicured fingernails are drumming. They'll drum until I comply.

I go—nine miles, 23 stop signs, 35 minutes.

I put my six month old daughter, my year-old and three-year-old sons, to sleep in my parents' home.

There is no one to consult.

I feel pressed to the point of destruction. This abrupt awareness of alcoholism falls swift and brutal just two months after my husband's death.

I want to scream where are the favored ones? Jennifer lives here. Celia is in nurse's training not six miles away. Call Franky home from the United States Air Force. Why can't they go, or come, or whatever?

I don't, of course. It's off to Alcoholics Anonymous.

The stories I hear of deprivation and depravity don't touch me. I have my own stories, now that I stop to think.

The jokesters make me feel physically ill. How dare they lighten and trivialize their damage. Sick humor, people laugh. I want to vomit. Not the bitter greenish yellow bile of morning sickness, but chunks of undigested beans and jalepeño peppers that burn my throat on the way up and cause my eyes to fill with tears that flood my face. Tears that mingle with the clear salty nasal flow that is not green and thick from a cold. If these secretions had a color it would be cobalt blue, for grief.

The AA meetings were successful. Daddy quit drinking, eventually. He got off and on the wagon for five months before he made sobriety a way of life.

Now we might become the substance of the image we had always appeared to be. I mean, we were the 4-H family of the year. The Kaufman Press newspaper photograph, with the article to prove it, is some place.

Daddy spearheaded a letter writing campaign to get alcohol ads off television because they made him salivate from desire. He never lost his desire. Just his mind. It was pickled. Sort of. At least that's how I interpret the doctor's highfalutin definition of Wernicke-Korsakoff Syndrome. The symptoms look a lot like Alzheimer's. But, unlike a child with a parent who has Alzheimer's, I'm not at risk. I don't drink alcoholic beverages.

Counting the Colorado River

The song says the sea refuses no river, but I know that is a lie. I've taken students to barrier island beaches and shown them sand from the Colorado River deposited miles from is current course because the sea choked on its delta and spit it back into the river's mouth until the river had no choice but to leave its bed and steal one from a smaller stream still currying ocean's favor. I've given students extra credit for keeping track of the number of times we cross the river between Houston and Austin. The faithless wishy-washy river that changes course around obstacles rather than persevere. I've taught them that a river carved the Grand Canyon by the gradually accumulated insult of carressing currents, but it is the lies that did the job. The constant barrage of lies until they seem to become the truth. Telling a child every morning and every night that you love him. Assuring him that you'll be there to protect him and nurture him. Returning his smiles and hugs. Feeding him. Tucking him in at night. Calming fears, soothing hurts, telling him he's a good boy. Proving to him he is worthy of love knowing that after years of fostering such a steady course he is likely to return to a world in which it all becomes lies.

JAMES HOGGARD

Parallel Wiring

The Indians in his line, along with his wife, taught him to keep whiskers off his face and secrets off his tongue, though he didn't always go that way.

—I can't stand chin-stubble, his wife said. I make him shave every day. I hate it when he thinks he might grow a beard. I don't like to itch—ever! she told her reading group. And I'm not a wart, she cried, but I'm going. I am. I don't understand, she said. He invited me last month and now he's backing out.

—Here, an amused friend said.

—No! No brownies, she begged. I've gained a mess of weight.

Listening from upstairs, I knew her man was warm for a toot. Money-making physicist now, he hadn't gotten tenure when the cutback shunted him into a new career. He was flying next week to New Orleans, for business, and the flesh of a woman who, he said, liked hairscratch sliding up and down her loins.

Smiling, he'd told me about her, saying:

—She's fair enough, I wouldn't kick her off my bed. And she even claims she hears tom-toms pounding out dreams in her head.

—I am! his wife shrieked. I'm going!

Knowing I'd heard that splintering timbre before, I remembered the crack in his own high voice, and I was having a bit of a dream myself: Neckties were dangling from tomahawks, then big winds came and blew those ties, now rainbows, up into huge arcs that fanned across a vast patch of laughing Apache sky, and the noise downstairs kept on.

JAMES HOGGARD

Points of Resistance

She cried by my apartment that she wanted to stay with me, she didn't want to go home, but I told her I had promised to get her back by eight-thirty, and crying, she kept saying she missed me.

Sweeping her up in my arms, I carried her to the door where, taking her, her mother asked:

—Why the hell is she crying?

—I think you know.

—Well, she said, she must've had a rotten time.

Kissing my daughter goodbye, I noticed my son, astraddle his bike, scowling in the carport's shadows.

—The next time you come, he said, I might still be out here.

As I hugged him he asked if I'd bring my new yellow cookie jar:

—If you two get back together.

Driving away, I saw he still hadn't moved. His arms tightly crossed, he sneered as his mother strode past him with a watering can for the plants. She'd told him yesterday, he'd said:

—I don't believe in priming the pump.

JAMES HOGGARD

Running the Peaks of the Moon

Early Easter morning, the wind up and the stirred air chilly, I ran from our colonía on a winding route out of town and up toward the Peaks of the Moon, the ridge of the mountain behind our place. I ran in fact on past the peaks, then finding at last the mountain's highest point, I climbed on top of a boulder there, and facing toward home, a thousand miles away, I spread my arms and chanted out loud new songs. The power of the cold wind gusting against me was thrilling, but knowing no gesture toward ecstasy would last, I knew when the rhythm of my breath began settling, it was time to climb down and run, time to shutter-step my way back down through splits in rock and low brush till I found the goat paths that would guide me back to the village and bridge I'd run through on my way here, but an impulse said to take a new way: run down the mountain's rocky ridge and run along the boulder stumps at the base of the jaggedly weathered eruptions called The Peaks of the Moon,

but the mountain, like the world below me in Ciudad Chihuahua, was ambiguous in its magnetic gestures. We were living in a country that often didn't work, and not far from here, in a place we could see from our yard, a company was dynamiting the mountain, but the place still had a powerful draw, though I resisted it when we first got there, and resisted it more when the outside water heater blew a ball of fire at me, but from where I was now I could see the enormous amoeba-shaped sprawl of the city, and inhaling the high desert's thin air, I improvised a zigzagging path as I let my gaze drift toward the wide, almost waterless riverbeds twisting below me,

so steeply below me, the dizzyingly distant flatlands a quick drop below me now, the abruptness of the drop shaking me out of the daydream I'd wandered into, having trusted my

105

feet to know where to shift pace and direction, but now I was sliding, slipping through a slurry of gravel, sliding now with little control toward the edge, toward a steep and sudden drop. I had to scramble back, had to clamber back up, no brush or trees to grab, and my feet no longer dependable guides, but I had to find a way to rise, and rise fast, at an ankle-breaking slant up the mountainside, higher up the wind-whipped slope—I couldn't retreat straight up, and the edge of the cliff was approaching.

And though I couldn't stop slipping, not yet, the daydreaming impulse returned and I found myself in the brilliance of the clear morning's glare remembering how the night before, when we'd come from a show downtown, I'd glanced at the twilight sky, too much glow to see many stars, but Venus was out, shining in her arrogant beauty brightly between buildings, just as she had the night before when we were driving two hundred and fifty miles through desert scorch, and the sand dunes resembled snowdrifts, and the daydreaming suddenly gone now, at least for awhile, I found myself leaving the edge of the cliff behind—the mountain was moving now inside me.

J. PAUL HOLCOMB

Negotiating with Igor

We freshmen were told to call the big guy, the black-headed muscleman with the Lil' Abner smile and the Arnold Schwarzenegger pecs, Igor. It seemed to fit, but I wasn't calling him Igor until I heard him say he wanted me to. And we were told to call the little guy, the fellow with acne and a smile always on his face, Raysir. I had no questions about that preference, and when I would see his flat top bobbing across campus I yelled, "Raysir" as loud as I could, and certainly before he would have time to bark, "Slime," and sneer his disgust at this fish.

My big brother told me always to walk to school with Jim. Jim too was a freshman but he was a football fullback, a talent resource to be respected by upperclassmen and, if it came to it, a good ally. And my big brother told me to accommodate upperclassmen, but not to let them steal from me.

After school one day, Jim and I went to the movie, walked home afterward. Dark surrounded us as Igor pulled up in his pickup and offered us a ride home. Once we were in the truck Igor said he needed some writing paper, asked me if I had any in my notebook. I said I didn't. Igor didn't seem annoyed but he did miss the turn toward the neighborhood where Jim and I lived. He drove out of town, down a deserted road and stopped. He ordered us out of the car, then got himself out. He walked toward my friend, pretended to launch a haymaker toward Jim, who immediately fainted as Igor pulled the punch.

That left me alone with Igor. He told me to stand in front of the headlights and drop my pants. I asked why and Igor said he had a cherry bomb (a popular firecracker) and he wanted to see how far it would blow my rectum apart. I told him that I lied, I really did have paper and he could have all he wanted. My nemesis with the chiseled body ignored me, said for me to drop my pants. I said I didn't want to, closed my eyes and waited for disaster. When nothing happened I peeked and saw that Jim had revived. Igor was standing over him, making sure he was all right. We all got back in the pickup. Igor drove us home and refused my repeated offers of paper.

Two weeks later I was told that Igor and Raysir fought. Raysir was no bigger than I was, and I was surprised to hear Igor had cut him with a broken beer bottle. I would have thought Raysir to be the one to arm himself in order to have a fighting chance. But then, I never did understand about Igor, Raysir, hazing, and cherry bombs. Heck, I even had to look "rectum" up in the dictionary.

Lupe's Candy

Jesús was glad when Lupe went into the candy business, figuring it would keep her out of his hair.

Tío Rogelio suggested it last Cinco de Mayo at the family dinner, topped off by Lupe's pralines. "Carita," he said, "you could make money with these," and everyone agreed.

They were chewy pecan pralines, but with a different taste. Lupe never told anyone her secret ingredient, but once Jesús popped in unexpectedly and saw her adding cayenne. "Now I know what gives it a bite!"

She glanced up sharply, wiping damp strands from her forehead. "You don't know nothing! It isn't always the same. Sometimes it's one thing, sometimes another."

Lupe began to devote her days, morning till night, to making pralines. Rogelio arrived with a basket of pecans, and Jesús and his friend Ángel were summoned to shell them.

Soon after, Rogelio brought a flyer he had made, offering "Lupe's Delicious Candy. Dirt Cheap."

Lupe sent Jesús to get five hundred copies made. Jesús grumbled but Ángel reminded him it was a small sacrifice to keep Lupe out of their business, which wasn't always strictly legal.

That was before Lupe instructed them to deliver the flyers door-to-door all over the Project. "Don't waste none of them," she warned, as if able to read their minds. "If you throw any away, I'll know."

"This is getting out of hand," Ángel grumbled. "We got to put a stop to this." They were taking a break over a *cerveza* at Lalo's Ice House, but not before they distributed every last flyer. When Lupe said I'll know, somehow she did.

An idea occurred to Jesús. "I *could* tell everyone what her secret ingredient is. That ought to slow 'er down."

Except that he spoke too loudly, and word must've reached Lupe on the wind, because the very next batch was different. Good, but different. And a little green.

It took Jesús several days to catch Lupe in the act to confirm his suspicions: she had switched to jalapeños as her secret ingredient.

She faced him down, little black eyes glinting like darts. "You blab this around, bucko, I'll be all over you like gnats on a jackass!"

Then she dispatched him to deliver her candy.

"This calls for desperate measures," Ángel told him. "It's time to call in the law. I think the Health Department'll want to know she's operating a bakery out of her kitchen."

Jesús, mindful of several outstanding warrants, was not in favor of involving the law. But he was at a breaking point. He rose from his customary seat at Lalo's and announced, "Okay, but I ain't going to be around when the law shows up, man."

But again, his voice must've carried back to Lupe, because the day before the Health Department official was to show up–he was only Hector Mendoza, from down the block–Lupe abruptly went off to Rogelio's place close to the Border. And Jesús heaved a sigh that the whole episode was over.

But on the morning Hector came, Lupe was back, and before Jesús and Ángel could make an escape, she threw open the door to the law. "Come in, boy. Have some candy."

Jesús and Ángel fled to the curb, where they waited for the verdict, hoping Lupe's fine would be steep enough to run her out of business.

Hector stayed far too long, and Jesús's bony behind was rebelling against the concrete. When Hector finally emerged, smiling, he carried a large bag. From the way Lupe waved goodbye, Jesús was certain her fine wasn't nearly big enough.

He rose to meet the food cop. "You bust her, man?"

Hector was munching on a praline. "Naw, I got her fixed up. Alicia, down at the office, she'll take her completely off

110

the computer. Won't nobody bother her about permits or taxes or nothing."

Anger rose in Jesús like hot lava. "What's the matter with you shit? Can't a man trust the law to do anything? That woman in there's a criminal, man. She needs to be shut down."

But Hector only grinned and extended his sack. "Chill out. Have a praline."

"Yeah," said Ángel, the traitor, who had already helped himself. "No need to get unstrung, man."

Jesús took a praline, eventually deciding he'd overreacted. Soon the three settled on the curb and ate the whole bagful.

Later, when Jesús's head cleared, he figured it out. "We've been duped, man." He grabbed Ángel's arm and hauled him back inside, where, under the sink they found a stash of tubercles of mescal from Rogelio's ranch.

Ángel faced him in defeat. "Hell, man. We haven't been duped; we've been *doped*."

Jesús shrugged and turned away. "Oh well then, never mind."

The Imán Stone

Ordinarily Rosa was not gullible. She didn't believe in most of the potions and charms La Curandera doled out. But when she was visiting in Laredo she chanced upon a woman selling the only true talisman: the Imán Stone, in a little red woolen bag, with a pamphlet of instructions that cost extra. Naturally she snapped them up and knew that her worries about Refugio's philandering were over.

Everyone knows the Imán Stone is where the body of Christ rested for three days after being taken from the cross. The pamphlet explained why the Stone was magic. Godfrey of Bouillon discovered its power in the Tenth Century when he led the First Crusade to Jerusalem. When all seemed lost, he went to Christ's sepulchre and begged the Lord's help. A voice whispered that he should carry a piece of the Stone upon which Christ had lain. He did and defeated the infidels. However, the Crusaders who followed him paid no attention to the Stone, and so they ultimately lost the Holy Land.

When Rosa returned to Pharr, following pamphlet instructions, she waited until Friday, then took the Stone to church, lit two candles near it, sifted salt on it, put it in holy water, and read aloud from the pamphlet: "I baptize you in the name of God the Father, God the Son; you will be my fortune and bring me good luck."

Then she knelt and said the "Our Father" before returning home by way of H.E.B.'s grocery, where she bought a sack of wheat. Back home, she took out the pamphlet and chanted, "Beautiful mineral and enchanting Imán Stone, who went about with the Samaritan, to whom you gave beauty, good luck and a man. I put wheat on you so that Refugio will be my faithful husband."

She bathed the Stone in consecrated wine, drank the wine, then put the Stone into the bag, sprinkling wheat into it.

That was on Friday. On Saturday night Refugio ran off with Mariann Murphy, from their old high school class. Old Man Murphy was the Assistant Principal, and everyone knew what a temper he had. Rosa could imagine the fit he threw when he learned that his daughter had disappeared with Refugio—not that Rosa blamed Mariann. When Refugio set his sights on a woman, he was irresistible.

Neither did she blame Refugio. Womanizing was his nature. No, the fault was hers. She must have done something wrong. She had taken some shortcuts, not thinking they were necessary. But obviously the Stone demanded complete compliance. She went to La Curandera and made several costly purchases: minute portions of gold dust, silver dust, copper dust, coral dust, and a special wheat which La Curandera said was much better than what you get at H.E.B.'s.

Back home, she waited for the arrival of Friday, when once more she took out the red woolen bag and began reading from the pamphlet, addressing the Stone.

"I put gold on you for my treasure, silver for my house, copper for the poor man, coral so that you remove from me evil and envy, and wheat, so that Refugio will be my faithful husband."

Again she bathed the Stone in wine and drank the wine, returning the Stone and its offerings to the bag.

On Saturday Refugio returned home. Technically it was Sunday morning, about three o'clock. He was drunk, and as was the case when he was soused, he was meaner than a javelina in heat. He stalked into their bedroom and flipped on the light, glaring down at her and bellowing so loud that everyone in the Project could hear.

"Where's my supper, lazy bitch?" He grabbed her by the hair and dragged her from the bed. She cried out in pain as she hit the floor.

113

Apparently Refugio had forgotten that he had been gone for a whole week. But Rosa had not, and owning the Stone gave her a certain daring she could not otherwise have mustered. Before he could strike her, she managed to wriggle free. She ran to the bed and drew the red bag from under her pillow. Taking out the Stone, she hurled it at Refugio. It struck him in the forehead, and he roared out, enraged.

Rosa leaped into the center of the bed and pointed a warning finger. "Don't touch me, Refugio! You've been hit by the Imán Stone, the real thing. You're going to die for sure!"

Refugio sobered in an instant and staggered out, mumbling, "Gotta wake Father Ignacio–beg for absolution, quick!"

Meanwhile Rosa retrieved the Stone, lit a candle to La Virgen and burned the pamphlet to ashes.

————

Incantations to the Imán Stone used in this story are the authentic ones actually used by believers in the Stone's power.

GRETCHEN LONG JAMESON

Me and Momma

In the late summertime, me and momma sleep on the front porch because it gets so hot inside our little house. We just have to be out where we can feel the night breeze. We pull the mattress to the far edge of the porch, so we can look up at the stars while momma tells me stories before sleep. Momma tells me the stars are dreams, and if I pick out one some day that star might fall, and I will get my dream. I love to listen to momma's gentle voice as I lie there. I can smell the soap, and starch smell of her washing and ironing clothes; her skin is soft and clean.

There are millions of stars, and it feels as though they've all fallen on top of me, like when my momma makes the bed with me in it. Momma snaps up the sheet and it balloons out, then slowly drops down exactly neat and straight to cover my whole body; the air presses cool against my skin as it's pushed out from underneath the wide, flat sheet. Momma is the only person who can do that, I've tried, and the sheet always lands crooked, or doesn't open up to make that wind as if I'm flying.

Momma falls asleep; her breath is quiet and even. A star falls across the light-sprinkled black sky, and I think of someone being happy somewhere. I move closer to momma, so I can feel her warm skin next to mine. We rest underneath a star sheet, me and momma, together.

GRETCHEN LONG JAMESON

Fireflies

We run across the dusky field to the edge of the woods, our grip tight around the Mason jars with ice pick-punched holes in the metal lids. Panting, the three of us pause, and turn to look back at the farmhouse. Yellow light streams through the small four-square-paned windows onto the clay road below. The TV is loud, and our parents' voices louder still, grow distant. The thin broken strain of words is carried up and away in the air until all we hear are the crickets and frogs calling to each other in their hidden world. The warm wind brushes the long dry grass at our feet; the sound of its rustle calms us, and urges us forward. We turn to face the woods and enter. My brother goes in first. My sister follows next, then me. I stay close to my brother. We run through the trees laughing and waving our arms. It is darker underneath the thick canopy, but they are not here yet, darkness has not completely fallen. As night descends, we stand close together looking out, our eyes vigilant of first sight.

"There, I see one there!" My sister and I turn to look, and see nothing. My brother says, "I saw one, really."

"Shh. Quiet!" my sister says.

We stand as still as we can, holding our breath. My heart races as I listen and watch for animals through the darkness. I can see the little lights in my own eyes like when I squeeze them shut tight. The air so black it covers me in blindness. I open my eyes wider, blinking to clear them. Then they begin. First one, then another, split-second flashes dance through the air.

Visitors to a secret world, we are surrounded by tiny flying stars, and I wonder at the sight of them. They are precious, carrying their own light to guide them, to guide others to them. An unspoken communication I have never seen before, but somehow know. I watch as my brother and

116

sister reach to catch the fireflies, being careful not to damage their fragile bodies. I see one in front of me, and reach out my hands to cup around the light. I miss it.

My brother comes to show me one he has caught. He opens his finger cage; a round prison, and I see the light inside. The lantern illuminates the insect, spindly and black, ugly against the miraculous light. My brother transfers the firefly into my hands. The firefly bumps, and lands around the inside of my palms and fingers, crawling and stopping, fluttering its wings against my skin. Squatting down to the ground, I put the tiny insect into my open jar, and quickly screw the top back on.

We run through the underbrush catching them. More and more have come, and I have become expert at trapping and containing the insect with the luminous cargo. It is a race to see who can get the most. I want to have a jar full of light that I created all myself.

There are fewer now. It is getting late. We hear the voices of our parents calling us to come out of the woods, and back across the field. We have to leave; the dance is over. We walk across the field with lit jars in hand. Our bodies sweaty and sticky and mosquito-bitten, we are happy to have been free in a world where we seem to have fit.

On the way back home to the city, I lie across the bench seat of our station wagon; my sister and brother sleep on top of me like toppled dominoes. I look down at my firefly jar on the floor of the car, the tiny lights blinking and swirling around, but they are getting dimmer, moving slower.

I want to turn back. I want to roll down the car window, and open my jar and free all the fireflies, but I know it is too late. My brother and sister would say I am silly to worry about such things, and I should have known. I have to lie here and watch as the jar slowly goes dark, then black as we reach our house in the city.

RAMONA JOHN

Gentle Ben

When the phone rang in the kitchen that Saturday morning, Ellie shut off the vacuum and sighed. Probably some salesman.

"Hello, Ellie." Although it had been fifteen years, she knew his voice.

"Ben! I can't believe it. For heavens sake, where are you?"

He said he was back in town, and asked to see her that night.

"I'd love that! Come about seven, and I'll fix dinner." I'll wear blue, she thought. He loved blue. "Oh, and Ben, I live in the country now. Take Anderson Road . . . "

"I know where you live, Ellie." he murmured.

She glanced at the hall mirror before answering the doorbell that evening. Not bad for thirty-five. Of course, she didn't look like the girl he'd remember.

Ellie hated thinking of the past. Dear, sweet Ben. They'd dated since high school, but something kept postponing their marriage, and years passed. Finally, that last summer they set a wedding date and mailed invitations.

It never happened. She'd been so stupid. A ball-player came to town, and she fell wildly in love. When he moved on in two weeks, so did she, leaving Ben a note. Three months later, the ballplayer beat her up, ending their great romance.

When Ellie came home, Ben was gone, but no one ever knew where. The broken ribs from the baseball player taught her what Ben's gentleness meant to her, and too late, she knew she really loved him.

Ellie opened the door. She'd forgotten how big he was. Ben looked at her a moment, then enveloped her in a hug.

Ellie's eyes filled with tears. "Oh, Ben," she said, her head buried against his shoulder.

He bent to whisper in her ear, "Shh, Ellie. I'm here now. I'll make everything all right."

Just then, the phone rang. She wanted to ignore it, but she'd never been able to do that.

"Ellie, thank heaven you're there. It's Sam Parsons."

"Why, sheriff . . ." Ellie began.

"Listen to me. You remember Ben Coleman?"

"Of course," Ellie said. "He's here now. What's this..."

"Oh, God. Get out of there. Go, right now. He's there to kill you, Ellie. We're on our way, but it'll take a few minutes."

"Are you crazy? I can't believe this," Ellie sputtered.

"His shrink just called from California. Ben escaped two days ago from a hospital for the criminally insane out there. He'd been locked up for ten years."

"No! Gentle Ben? He wouldn't..." Ellie's voice was shaking.

"He slit three women's throats before they caught him, and the doctor thinks he's coming for you next." He paused. "They were all named Ellie."

Ice seemed to form in her spine and spread throughout her body. She carefully replaced the receiver, and turned toward the back door.

Ben was standing there, smiling. "Leaving me again?" He shook his head and reached inside his jacket. "Ah, Ellie," he said tenderly.

LISA KAHN

Eurydice

When his eyes could almost recognize shapes and colors (after the trauma of stumbling for days in the darkness of a thousand abysses that had trapped them both) he grabbed her hand—the left one—pressed it against his lips and spoke (while his gaze was still averted to obey the divine command):

"One thing only promise me! Don't sing! You have no right to do it! No right! You comprehend?"

His voice kept growing: "You must not! Do you hear?" His words imploring wrapped her in a garment of yielding; she needed but to nod in the dark, to whisper "yes" but she kept silent (and it screamed in her: why the return to earth if I am not allowed to sing? How icy I'll feel in the light!)

And his renewed command: Don't dare to sing!"

Now roaring towards her a thundering avalanche approaching closer and closer.

Just as the snow mass rolled to touch her feet to bury her she shouted—shouted with all the vessels of her fear-tormented flesh, with feet, fingers, hair and heart:

"I also want to sing!"

He turned his head and his disgusted ghastly gaze hit her—then with her throat already covered by snow—her breathing ceased.

Left Without a Trace

Wham. Wham. Sandra dodged the ball and dashed toward the front porch stoop.

"I got . . . you, . . ." her nine-year-old son sang out as he tackled her on the second step.

"So you have. " She laughed, ruffling his hair. "Come on, Davy. Time to do homework. "

His freckled face screwed up in a grimace, reminding her painfully of his father. "Mom, do I have to? I can do it later, can't I?"

"Nope." She took his hand, leading him onto the porch and inside the three-room duplex where he grudgingly sat at the kitchen table and opened his books.

Sandra squeezed into the tiny adjoining kitchenette and started on the tuna noodle casserole that was a Thursday night staple. They ate the leftovers every Friday night. Hot dogs on Saturday and so on. Their unvaried menu was a reflection of their life since Chad left them—or rather disappeared from their lives without a trace. No messy divorce. No custody battles over their son. Also no alimony. Just this feeling of being deserted, wondering what she did wrong, feeling as if some defect within her drove him away.

Almost one year had passed. A year in which she grew reconciled to his abandonment. Accepted that he wasn't sick somewhere needing her, kidnapped or dead. Accepted that he didn't want either one of them. Not her and not their son, sensitive and intelligent, made in his image so much that sometimes looking at him or listening to him talk sent shafts of pain barreling through her chest.

Chad's letter arrived three weeks after he left. The paper was now worn and tear-stained, its message rehearsed and spun into the web of their lives:

Sandra,

I left because I couldn't stand the pretense. Our marriage was a prison, and the family you desired created the bars that locked me into a job I didn't want and an image of your choosing. Stop calling the hospitals and the police. Call off the investigators. Accept that I'll never be back. If it helps, pretend I'm dead. You're so good at the game, it shouldn't be hard.   Chad

As much as she would have liked to, she couldn't deny that the letter was real. The handwriting was Chad's and the postmark Zurich. But such cruelty from the man she thought of as her tender, unassuming husband was new. When had his heart grown so cold? How? Lord, she prayed, give me a clue.

Had she been so different from the other wives she knew? Or was it that Chad hadn't wanted what everyone else had? Now she'd never know. Neither would her son who assumed some of the guilt, just as she did, for boxing Chad into a corner and driving him away.

The silence haunted her. Why hadn't he said something earlier? Was she the one pretending or had it been him? She truly believed that Chad loved her, that theirs was a happy family. Tomorrow, she and Davy could trust again, but not yet . . . not today.

Only last night, Davy asked, hiccupping back the sobs that shook him. "Will Daddy ever come home?"

Sandra gathered him in her arms. "I don't know, honey. Someday though, I promise you, everything will be better."

"How soon, Mom? Most all my friends have daddies."

"Shh . . . darling. After the trees have lost all their leaves and are laid bare, they winter the cold harsh winds, rain and snow, and their roots dig deep into the earth for nourishment, then spring always comes. "

Davy's hand slipped into hers. "Mom, when does spring come?"

122

KIMBERLY KING

Female Anatomy

He touches my spine while I brush my teeth. His forefinger finds the soft notch between the bones in my lower back.

"This is the spot," he says. "Between L4 and L5—you draw a line from the iliac crest."

He explains that spinal taps are easier to perform on infants because their bones are still soft. I spit white foam into the sink and wipe my mouth with the back of my hand. I ask him if he is afraid of paralyzing a baby. He tells me he is the best in his class. He tells me there were no red blood cells in his last sample.

He gives me bi-weekly breast exams. He inspects my body an inch at a time with his hands, his mouth, his tongue. He possesses a deep knowledge of the female anatomy. He discovers my cervix with the tip of his index finger. He pushes upwards and tells me what he finds. I pull his hand away and press it to my stomach. Don't.

In a panic I ask him to find my liver. I have had too much to drink.

"It may be enlarged," I say.

He hides his smile and tells me to lie back. He lifts my shirt and pushes on my abdomen. He looks straight ahead and palpates.

"It's fine," he says. "You don't feel anything unless it's abnormal."

Drunk and unconvinced, I begin to cry for my lost organ.

"Here," he says. "Here are your kidneys. And your ovaries. And your heart."

"Find more," I say.

He tells me that in anatomy lab they could not find a cadaver with a uterus. He tells me 4:5 women who donate their bodies have had hysterectomies. The students will complete their studies on female pigs.

"It's not the same thing," I tell him.

"Of course not," he says. "But we have to take what we can get. Everyone is disappointed."

I imagine him among the other students. I picture him lifting sheet after sheet with growing disappointment. He catalogues the organs without touch. He moves between open bodies.

MAXINE KOHANSKI

The Way We Are

Dear Rob,

It's difficult to believe that twelve years have passed since you and your new bride left for Indiana to begin your final year of college. I watched as all of your belongings, the furniture you had worked so hard to purchase for your new home, was packed into a U-Haul. I was so proud of you. When it was packed, my eyes brimmed over; life would never be the same. Your sister graduated from A&M around the same time and took an assignment in the Middle East. I watched her walk the ramp to the plane and felt any minute she would turn around and come back. We would go home and life would be the same as before. But she didn't. And your young bride called from a pay phone and cried, "I want to come home." I walked in a trance for the first six months and cried continuously. Losing the three of you was like the lights had gone out.

One night I was awakened to see your sister standing in the bedroom door. She walked to my side of the bed, leaned over, her hair falling down, touching my face. It was a dream but it felt so real. She was in the Persian Gulf, though not in the military; I worried about her. I'm still struck by the fact that your fourteen-year-old brother brought me back to reality. We were in church one Sunday morning and I was in tears again. He reached across your dad and took my hand and in a soft sad voice said, "Mom, I'm still here." I broke into tears again. I couldn't answer. For the past six months I had been so different; I had shut him out. Leaving the church we walked with our arms around each other. I knew I would continue to miss you both and worry about your sister's safety because of the problems in the Gulf, but life is filled with changes, and I realized before long you would come home and that soon your younger brother would be old enough to venture out. I would have the same feelings of loss. I also knew our family shared a strong bond and we'd be together as much as time allowed, because that's the way we are.

Love Mom

KAREN O. KRAKOWER

Dream House of a Saboteur

All I asked for was a chance at a blueprint, schematic etchings of our own design. I said, let's shed the burden of right angles, throw out all the old rules. You said, let's take turns at the drafting table, and see what this plan of ours divines.

I said, let's start by finding some mutual ground, clear it of rocks and roots we might stumble on. You said, let's not get carried away here, throw our backs out. After all, we're bound to fumble and fall anyway. Might as well have something to blame it on.

So I said, then let's lay a foundation of flawless stone so thick that earthquakes will think twice before striking. You said, hell, let's jack hammer the damn thing before we get started, so we'll know where the cracks are when the walls come crashing down.

Then let's shed all convention, no walls at all. One less thing to come between us. No walls, just beams and a canopy roof whose grace shields us from what falls from the sky.

You said, let's rethink the roof idea . . . all it takes is one good rain for its inevitable collapse under its own weight, surely to kill us in our sleep.

Finally you erased even the blue off the print, wadding up the etchings of our own doomed designs. I said, please, let's draw us a door before you sabotage us too. You said, let's shed the whole *us* thing, in case it fails, or worse, succeeds. I'll always lust for demolition more than I desire to break ground.

126

WILLIAM H. LAUFER

Change of Skin

I often think that the ultimate object of human fear is beauty: when it erupts in our lives it disarms, it ravishes and brings us to our knees.

Abscission begins now, a new carpet against old erosions. Leaf fall tells on the higher ground, and the pattern slides down into the swales and runnels. This tapestry—its perception—overwhelms and seasons memory with ache.

Gibbous moon leans into her next season, sinking to join the waking world where I take comfort. Yet, dispersal and fragmentation blow together with the wind, leasing comforts, the small and the grand, into scarcity. The nymphs are departed: by what must we live now—how—to weave another destiny out of this emptiness?

It is hard into midmorning and Sunday ritual when Pan-shout splinters the forest stillness, echoes down against the gentle hillsides, harrows tithe-payers and other fleet shapes fleeing surprise and fear as though these were plague. The shout scatters disorder like old zinc pennies flung into the shrub and scrub pines, to vanish eventually in the shadows—expired currency in any venue. Now language passes away and meaning with it, while depth and vision persist, ineffable. I hear pandemonium.

Why, brother, why this hail to me now, out of season, out of context, with no hoof prints in my raked and tended ground? I hear only your pagan call, only the summons to which I respond unwittingly: Wait for me. Here.

WILLIAM H. LAUFER

Kumar the Blind Speaks

You ask me how I envision you. I see you wholly as the scent of citron misting across the desert of my mind at dusk. I see your fragrant hair as flame pluming from the surface of the sun at sunrise—burnt auburn, burning orange. Your fingers: pincers of appetite refusing to be stilled that, crablike, bring my fingers to know the columns which are your thighs—complex surfaces, hot marble. I see your voice as the blue tongue that spreads my lips apart, teases my eyelids, and raises me into the full light of your presence. Unseen, you have looted flesh from my body and its soul. I demand reparation. How can it be that there is more of you for me to see? Show yourself to me that I again may be whole.

You ask what my dream was. I dreamed of you sitting, disheveled, laughing, your bared thigh pressed to my thigh. Autumn sunlight passed low from the Kerala hills through our latticed window, crossed your twin breasts and mine, and joined us, light and shadow.

I wrote these lines in the six-hundredth year of the Christian era, when I worked as apprentice to the Sanskrit poet Amaru, and when I lived as the beloved of Rajam, his wife.

VANESSA LEVRIER LEGGETT

Wake-up Call

I think I had come to believe that she couldn't die. It didn't matter that she was my mother and, in every sense, a very sick woman, rotting from the inside out. I imagined that, because neither heaven nor hell would have her, she'd perpetually roam the earth in some sort of reverse purgatory where the job was to purge herself of all kindness by tormenting unsuspecting souls; like her family, a flock of fools who suffered from fifties sit-com delusions—replete with a sound card of sinister laughter in the background—that a mother should be loving and kind. Shit.

So when my sister called from the hospital and said, "Amos? I think this is it," I almost didn't believe her. But then, you have to know this particular sister. Malachi, like me, *never* exaggerated. And I can say "never" because it's the damned truth. That's why when she said she believed it was time, I thought for a moment that they'd probably already pronounced Mother dead; that Malachi wouldn't say she had died until the last spadeful of earth had showered the casket. It *had* to be real.

I drove to the University Medical Center that night. It was raining. Naturally. The windshield wipers' rhythmic cleaving of water pummeling my windshield lulled me into a trance. Had she truly always been a wretch? Was there ever a time that the hand that slapped me senseless so often actually caressed me? Then a montage played across my consciousness, and I saw her. Young, with milky white skin and flowing red hair emblazoned by the sun, lifting a baby, tickling him. It was me. I was grasping for her hair and blissfully gurgling.

"I love my baby Mo," she'd said. And it seemed like I knew, and that I loved her too. Then her tear splashed on my little nose and I looked up to see hurt in her eyes. Suddenly I envisioned what she saw. A little redhaired freckled girl crying in a corner. A man, faceless, approaching her, unbuckling his pants. Kneeling before her.

I heard a horn and the image went white. A prism of headlights appeared on my windshield and I was back. I realized I was crying. Sad for her. Jesus. Other memories flickered, both good and bad. Were any of them real? Or was my mind reshuffling its miserable deck in a last-minute attempt to make sense of it all?

After parking, I stepped through the sliding glass doors into the frigid, sickly sterile world of the hospital. I hate the way hospitals smell. The PA system pinged, paging doctor after doctor. When I heard "Code Blue," my stride tripled and I jammed my hand in my pocket to fish out the room number Malachi had given me. The corridor's glassy clean tiles seemed endless as I wove through what was like a slow-motion carnival: patients pushing IV trees, nurses wheeling carts, and the occasional doctor standing, flipping a chart.

I got to her room, heart pounding and out of breath. No crash cart. No one. A sheet shrouded her body. No. I scanned the screen for vitals. She was alive. Or was I hallucinating, having some kind of selective perception? Could I actually have wanted her to live?

I slowly slid the sheet down to her waist. Her head was facing away from me toward the picture window, where she gazed through the tears of the rainy night. Then she turned to me and I gasped. Her complexion was youthful and radiant, and as she whispered my name, her jade eyes were wet with sorrow and compassion. I fell at her bedside—pressing my face into the mattress that smelled of urine and detergent—and sobbed. I felt her hand touch the top of my balding head and without looking up, I reached forward and her hands clasped mine. I rose and our eyes met. Mother and son. In this cold place where it seems all life begins and ends, a warm current of understanding flowed between us and all the pain of forty years seemed to wash away.

Catching my breath, I started to tell her that I *did* love her. That I always had. That she was my mother, would always be my mother; and how sorry I was about everything.

The phone rang. We let it ring and ring and ring. But then I opened my eyes and I was in the darkness of my bedroom. Four o'clock in the morning. I grabbed the phone. It was Malachi.

Lunch Break

There were no green pastures for this old mare. Neglect showed in her matted mane, dull coat, and in her spiritless eyes as she plodded round and round the corrugated-metal, makeshift sugar mill. Harnessed to a beam, she was forced to walk a narrow path, unable to deviate to the left or right.

The other end of the beam was attached to a post in the center of the circular mill and as the horse walked, her broad shoulders pulled it with her. This rotated two large-cogged gears that turned heavy crushers and grinders. In this manner the sugar-bearing juice was squeezed from the cane and streamed down a sluice into a syrup-encrusted bucket that sat on the ground

It was hard to tell which was more unkempt, the horse, or the man feeding the heavy canes into the mill. Both were sweating profusely as they worked under the unrelenting, blazing sun. A red bandanna tied around the man's forehead did little to keep the sweat from running down his face and darkening the straggles of gray hair that clung to his neck. His overalls bore the stains of his work.

The horse's pace never changed. Only when the bucket was full and the man shouted an order to her did she slow down and stop. He then carried the brimful bucket to a large oil drum into which he dumped the syrup.

The man pulled a watch from the back pocket of his overalls and, seeing that it was almost noon, unharnessed the horse. He led her to the shade of a nearby clump of trees and tethered her to a metal stake in the ground. Then he fetched a pail of water and placed it near her feet.

The horse watched as the man walked a short distance towards another clump of trees where he had left his lunch pail. He dropped to the ground beside the largest tree and leaned back against it. For a few moments he closed his eyes and listened to the buzzing of cicadas until he became aware of another sound. He glanced over at the horse and saw her kicking at the metal stake. He reached for his lunch pail and glanced again at the horse in time to see her rear up on her hind legs, once . . . twice . . . and then a third time. He saw the tether snap. Instantly, the mare took off for a nearby field at a fast trot that belied her age.

The man jumped up. "Come back, you goddamned nag," he screamed, but he was too old to chase after her. He watched her for a few moments and then sank to the ground thinking that sometimes he too would like to break away.

The horse kept going until she came to a dusty patch of ground where she stopped. She let herself down and rolled from side to side, arching and twisting her back, until she was covered with the sandy dirt. She lay there awhile, and then got up.

Slowly, she made her way back to the shady clump of trees, stopping now and then to nibble the few tufts of green grass that had survived the summer heat.

PEGGY ZULEIKA LYNCH

Keepers of the Word

Yes, we are the keepers, Edmund and I, of your words. We are framing them in black on white. They are formed and reformed, changing shapes between black notebook covers under plastic, into and out of "input" and "output" status.

But these words remain like soldiers marching in formation, quite like the West Point cadets in cadence. Whether together or apart, reassembled into one mass, destined as counterpoints, they perform their roles in whatever state, and always will remain in their grouping revealing their meanings.

Their rhythms tantalize, their melodies captivate, their meaning instill, and forever and ever their uniqueness will prevail. The authors, the poets, will pass on. There will be left behind these poems for posterity to contemplate, associate, catalogue and compare.

Bravo Prosperity!

PEGGY ZULEIKA LYNCH

Poet at Large

I feel my need to write, whatever I write, but particularly poetry comes from an inquisitive nature that constantly keeps me studying people. Against the hard sounding board of "why", I have internally questioned the varieties of human behavior. With this search has come understanding and an urgency to aid and improve differences. Most often I have attempted to express these with my words, even the delicate subtleties, and with intense desire to be a poet capable of hammering into readers' minds these captured moments of truths. The compliment that reaches deep into my soul's gratification is that one phrased similarly, "How did you know me so well, that you could write this poetry book about me?"

JEANETTE McSHERRY

Christmas in Old Town Spring
A Holiday Home Away from Home

Rebelling against obligatory purchases and Christmas lists, I plan to fill a few hours finding a few last-minute remembrances. Alone doesn't feel so lonely, hidden within the warm embrace of the crowd. Absorbing their laughter makes shopping an adventure. I discover a purple people-eater for my all-too-practical lover, and a hand-blown glass ornament for an aunt with hundreds already stored in her attic.

For once, being on my own in this far-away place works to my advantage. I can cover more ground alone, sweeping like a cool winter wind along the festive, busy streets where pedestrians have the right of way.

I still miss the traditional reminders of Christmas from my Yankee roots: sleigh riding and snow angels, footprints in the snow, and the fireside magic attached to winter cold. Smiling faces, holiday cheer, Christmas carols and handcrafted trinkets dull some small portion of the pain, turning homesickness into a storage chest of pleasant memories.

Nestled in a fragrant room of frankincense and myrrh, I sip gratuitous hot-spiced-cider as I browse each craftsman's wares. The bold Norwegian glass blower twinkles in my direction as he performs his art, weaving away my melancholy with his magic. I turn to see a child's face pressed against the shop's glass window—eyes filled with wonder as an intricate crystal angel is born.

Wonderful smells waft from the bakery. Stopping to sample a gingerbread delight, I watch a group of children flock to an authentic-looking Santa wearing Texas boots and a plaid flannel shirt. Red velvet and white fur trim has been sensibly exchanged for southern comfort.

Dabbing at my eyes, I hurry on, but Santa reaches out and takes my hand. "Merry Christmas," he says in an undeniable New England accent, his genuine smile an apt reminder of the reason for this season.

136

LIANNE ELIZABETH MERCER

Passions of Daughters

On the train to Mexico City, the small girl smiles from her daddy's lap. Turquoise and silver earrings jangle. White lace stockings end in dusty patent leather shoes. Soiled leg-o-mutton sleeves puff over plump arms. A torn, flowered pinafore strap dangles at her waist.

She climbs into the crowded aisle, wedges her foot against an orange plastic bucket holding a foaming jug of *pulque*, lifts from a basket a yellow-red-green-black striped *rebozo*, shrugs into it the way I wear remembered conversations with my father. She clutches the shorter left side of the *rebozo*, extends her right arm the length of the weave, flings the fringed end across her heart to her left shoulder.

Folds come undone. It falls away. My father survived the Depression, warned me that writing poetry would keep me poor, said I needed a profession to fall back on. The long right end slides down her round stomach. She tries again. And again. I admire her will. I wrote poems after work, never showed them to my father.

One time, the flung *rebozo* suits her. She clasps her fingers, grins at her daddy, at me. My father died before my first poem was published. The little girl licks *pulque* bubbles from the jug, giggles into her daddy's lap, scatters yellow and green, wraps her legs around his waist, shuts her eyes. His old black coat shines her shoes. He pats her back. She sleeps.

I know the seduction of closed eyes and safe arms. Through dirty windows, green fields rush past like years, purple-pink-orange clouds dazzle. I sip lukewarm beer and lean into the hard seat, into my father's words. I fold days to show red, snow on mountain peaks defying the sun, blue forget-me-nots. I fling colors over my shoulder. Take out pen and paper. Begin this poem.

137

LIANNE ELIZABETH MERCER

Seeking the Rainbow Way

Vinnie and I are in the ballroom of a posh Houston hotel along with two hundred questing women. We perch on metal folding chairs drinking decaffeinated coffee, waiting for Ronald the Cheyenne Medicine Man to show us the Rainbow Way. Trouble is, he's fogged in in Dallas.

I've spent the morning half-listening to Ronald's henchwomen talk about disease and energy fields, and half-watching Vinnie sketch rainbows and some of the women. Bored eyes. Earlobes drooping with diamonds or turquoise. Why are they here? Seeking inner peace? Something to tell their friends? I'll get names and phone numbers. Interview them. Write a story. Deduct the workshop fee. I'm a journalist. Vinnie's the one who wanted to come. She's an artist, and she wants to learn how to draw the colors right out of herself, like the brochure promises.

Ronald appears during lunch. He gulps a tuna sandwich at the table where his book, *Seeking the Rainbow Way*, is for sale. He's short, wears a crew cut, glasses, an expensive black suit and an airport aura. After lunch, he tries to accomplish in ten minutes what he usually takes a morning to do—set up a mood. Some women lean forward, listening. Others drum manicured nails on notebooks. I want a campfire smoking with buffalo chips, stars, pine trees whispering in the wind.

He says we have the answers we seek inside us; we need to ask the right questions. I wonder why this medicine man with a Ph.D. in education from Harvard is telling tribal secrets to urban women. At ninety dollars a head, he's making a bundle, but surely there's more to it. Will he hold something back like Audrey did when she copied grandma's recipe for sour milk cake? Ronald says he's telling us about the Rainbow Way because it's time to heal the cynicism of the world. I'm surprised he answers my mental question. Maybe it's one of the right ones. Vinnie sketches him with feathered headdress and loincloth, his foot on an ax.

At our first break, while I'm sniffing granola bars to find those with real chocolate, while a woman in an orange caftan tells me she's here because she's desperate to find help for her alcoholic son, Vinnie shows Ronald her sketch. Back in our seats, she says he told her she's stuck in her stereotypes. She draws another ax. Ronald says we should look beyond appearances to see a person's aura. Vinnie says, "He's the only one here wearing black."

"The Rainbow Way begins with black, with the absence of light," Ronald says.

I feel my scalp prickle. His hands are square and strong. Short nails. A century ago those hands might have yanked our colors from us. I want him to touch me, and I want to run.

"God is expanding inside your mind, inside your spirit, inside your body," Ronald says. I get this sensation like kernels of corn on a hot roasting ear. My fingers tingle. I quit taking notes, watch his face. Imagine him in the medicine lodge, sweat coating his body. I bet everyone in the Dallas airport gave him a wide berth. I notice Vinnie has quit drawing axes and is staring at him. This room is suddenly warm. My eyelids are sweating.

The woman next to me fans herself with a brochure, says "I notice everyone's wearing their turquoise. I'll have to buy some and get spiritual." I wonder how it would feel to strangle her with her pearls.

Suddenly Vinnie leaps from her chair and rushes Ronald. "What are your colors?" Definitely not the right question. She yanks at his tie and pulls his shirt open before his henchwomen shove her away, before I reach her. "Fraud!" Vinnie yells. Murmurs behind us escalate into shouts.

"I've got her," I tell the women. "We're leaving."

"He hasn't told us anything we didn't already know."

"I'm sorry," I tell Ronald. "Vinnie's a good artist. She wanted to learn from you."

His glasses are askew on his face; his muscular chest heaves. "She learned only what she already believed."

"Psycho-Indian babble," says Vinnie.

I propel her toward the door. Some women give us thumbs up. Others ignore us as though we are roaches who've crawled from the snacks.

"And you," Ronald calls. I turn around. "Have you found what you came for?" He nods. Counting coup? An Indian playing an educator? Or the other way around?

Behind his head I see green and blue fingers of light. I feel tears on my cheeks, then hiccough and laugh.

Vinnie clutches my arm. "You all right?"

In the hallway, I still feel Ronald's gray eyes piercing my soul. I feel black dissolving into colors I didn't know existed. I tell Vinnie I'm fine.

Junie Marie and the Daytime Moon

"**H**ey, Granny, guess what? We learned all about the moon in Mr. Gillian's class today. We went outside and we could see the moon, in the daytime! Bet you didn't even know you can see it in the daytime, didya, Granny?"

"Humph. What I know, child, is that the devil sometimes interferes with God's business, and that I don't want you lookin' at any daytime moon. The Good Book makes it plain that the Lord made the sun to light the day and the moon to show the way at night. When it don't work that way, it's just old Satan monkeyin' around."

"But Granny, Mr. Gillian says we can see the moon at certain times of the day 'most all month long. 'Cept when it's close to time for the new moon, or right when there's a full moon. Don't you think that's somethin'?"

"The only thing I think about it, Junie Marie, is I don't want you a'gazin' at it. Like I said, it ain't natural, and it's the devil's work."

"But Granny, how come you don't believe Mr. Gillian? He's the teacher!"

"Oh, he's the teacher, all right." Granny scoffed testily. "Can't be more'n twenty-five or thirty. I reckon when he's lived as long as my Papa did, maybe he'll have some wisdom in him."

"What's Big Granddaddy got to do with it? I can't even remember him."

"Junie Marie, ever since I was knee-high to a grasshopper, Papa warned us 'bout lookin' at a daytime moon. He said it would cause all kinds of bad things to happen, and that we mustn't tempt the devil that way. I got to see just what he meant, too."

"What did he mean, Granny? What'd you see?"

"I seen poor old Levi Pickens go down to rack and ruin

141

in nineteen-ought-nine, and all because he took to lookin' at the sky with that old spyglass that come off his Uncle Zeb's fishin' boat. I wasn't more'n about five years old, but I remember old Levi studyin' that sky every time he could see a daytime moon. That very winter, mind you, Miz Pickens died of the flu. The followin' year, Levi's crops failed when ever'body else's did good. Then late in the fall, lightnin' struck his barn and killed his plow horses and both his milk cows. Papa said that just about finished old Levi off, and that it just goes to show you what lookin' at a daytime moon can do for a body."

Junie Marie sniffed the air in anticipation as Granny took a pan of gingerbread from the oven. She cut a hefty square, topped it with a dollop of home-churned butter, and placed it in front of her granddaughter.

"S'pose maybe this'll get your mind off foolish things for a bit?"

Junie Marie just nodded and poured a glass of milk for herself while her gingerbread cooled. She sat down to do her homework for Mr. Gillian's science class, a secret smile twitching the corners of her mouth as she considered Granny's funny superstitions.

Still, maybe she wouldn't look for those old daytime moons any more. No use taking chances.

REECE NEWTON

Ducky's Sweetpeas

Was I four or five? Hitler was just dead, what did I know? My sidewalk world was OK. Helping Ducky with her garden, I walked hand in hand with her to the lumber yard where she bought a piece of chicken wire. We carried it back all coiled tight, and then we tried to fix it on poles by her back porch, for sweetpeas to climb. The springy wire fought, wanted to stay coiled. Ducky worked above, her pale forehead beaded with sweat in the Texas spring, while I tried to hold the monster fast at the bottom, and stay shy of the sharp cutting wires.

Then a colored man walked by. Our big people called his people colored and taught us little people to. He walked in the street, not on the sidewalk, the way they always did, that was how it was, it was what I knew. Ducky knew what she knew: "Here," she called, "come help me with this chicken wire."

Silently over the curb, the sidewalk, the grass, he crossed raggedy into the back yard, removing his hat. Silently he listened to her instructions, then wrestled with the stubborn wire that wouldn't straighten but snarled, recoiled, struck; fanging four sharp scratches on the smooth chocolate arm, shockingly crimson drops quickly beading, running, drawing a gasp from me. In my sidewalk world, a skinned knee would bring tears, then Mamma's soothing, Mercurochrome, or the dreaded iodine with its skull and crossbones, and finally a bandage. "You're bleeding!" I piped, "Don't you want a band-aid?" His rheumy eyes, bordered yellow, riveted my white-boy blue ones a long instant, his face impassive, saying nothing. A sense of something not right stayed with me from that day, but years would pass for me to know that it would take more than band-aids to staunch the bleeding.

VIOLETTE NEWTON

The Resident Poet Contemplates an Anthology of Poetry

He contemplates the smoking cities of the soul, and he thinks,
of all words man has written since man's written these are the
few Time savored and so, saved. He scans them once again
and sifts of all but themes. What's there? Love's love, war's
war, Time's present, and paradise is always lost. He knows
the cost, what arrow thrusts once jolted every line to being,
yet he can hold the whole lot in his hand. His own notebooks
look thin and dog-eared on his desk. Inside, his poems show
where he's crawled with bloody hands up jagged mountains,
how he suffered in rare air and suffered beauty beyond daring.

When he is sifted to a spoonful or a cinder, he wonders if one
phrase of his will last. So what's the use? A man with half a
mind avoids such senseless slavery. He bends in pain. The
nail of poetry's driven through his heart. He wriggles like a
fly upon a pin. He reaches for his paper and his pen.

VIOLETTE NEWTON

We Came in, Laughing

We came in laughing, from our weekend, and the diningroom was crawling with caterpillars. We stood in the doorway and saw gray masses moving on curtains, up ceiling, down walls, slowly, hundreds of them together moving, moving slowly. The laughter we'd laughed a moment before shattered in our memory like glass, and truth went in like a knife. We could not leave, we could not walk away from this. "Newspapers," you said, your voice chilled with awe. I turned in relief at your order, the first step in making order for us. I brought papers and you worked, looking warily up, then covering table and cabinets and chairs, even floor. "Spray can," you whispered as if the moving mass could hear us. I brought it and you aimed, backing off, watching the gray worms fall, aimed again and came out of the cloud, to tie up your face, and all but your eyes, with a cloth. You aimed again and again through thickening fumes while I hovered near the door. When the work was complete, we went out in air to be away from that death.

More were outside, moving on trees, hundreds together, on walls, everywhere. Wordless, we looked, and wordless, we returned to the house. We searched all the rooms, gingerly opening curtains and drawers, scanning every wall, looking in closets. We had got to them before they came that far, for none were there. So we went back to bundle up newspapers, tiptoeing softly, looking ahead, looking behind. And outside again, you found port of entry, a spot where caulking around a low window had a small break, an opening so small, no one would have noticed. Gray creatures were still lined up before that spot like jets timed for takeoff on a busy runway.

You sealed the place and declared we were safe, but that night we tossed, sleeping little. And now, we shudder and wonder and dream of attack, we nightmare at trespass we hope we never may see, we shudder at ideas and armies that move in in silence through invisible openings we know must be there in the structures of our lives, of our states, of our land. We are watchful, we are wary, we are warned.

145

MICHAEL POEHLS

The Pigeons

The pigeons huddle together and murmur to themselves. Memories of death are on the wind, and pain and fear, as it blows cold and silent, having left the screams half a world behind. The pigeons guard their warmth like innocence as they gather their feathers around them, their soft, brown shields. Above, the trees embrace the wind and cry tears on its shoulders, in red, orange, and yellow trickling down onto the cage and the October ground, where the colors mix and march, single file, and sometimes in sad little swirling circles as they make their way across the grass to rest finally with their heads against the house, listening, listening.

Inside is the ticking of a clock. And a faucet drips on the porcelain, cold and hard, marking time in its own relentless way. The sun blows cold shadows onto the wall of the room where the old man sits, stonelike in his chair. The letter relaxes, wrinkled in his hands. He reads it for the third time, though he knew its words before he cut them free of the envelope. He lays the letter aside and breathes. It's been such a long time since he's breathed.

At his side are the pictures, and his soul aches. Pictures of smiles, and laughter, the boy and the girl. The girl with her baton. The boy with his pigeons. "Feed them while I'm away," the boy had said. "I'll set them free," the old man teased. "You can't set them free. They're pigeons. They always come home."

They always come home.

The old man climbs up from his chair and his legs drag him to the window where the sun is turning red. He will have to call the girl soon. She will call the others. Then they will all come, with their wet eyes and their wet hands, and their cakes and their casseroles. They will drink coffee, and pat his back, and they won't know what to say, so they will say they're sorry. And he won't know what to say, so he will say "Thank you", or maybe he'll just nod his head. Then they will leave, even the girl. Leave with the parson, and the Fletchers and Coles, and old Mrs. Smith. Old Mrs. Smith, who had told him not to worry about being alone.

"Children are like pigeons," she had said. "They always come home."

They always come home.

The wind calls to the old man and his tired legs answer. They pull him outside where the sun lays down and the pigeons whisper. The leaves cry out under his feet, and the birds crowd against the mesh as the old man's hand reaches in and curls gently around the first of the many. He holds the soft, warm body to his face, where it hears his prayer, and feels his tears. Then, with the fingers of his other hand, he bows the bird's head, and with a quick twist and a snap, releases its warmth onto the wind.

SHIRLEY COUVILLION-POWELL

Aftershock

In the midnight of her leaving, he waits for sleep, trying to forget the sound of a door slammed shut. He waits for the fade-out of ocean music and love's whispers muffled in wet sand. Waits to forget the sins and omissions of jeweled days and jasmine nights and heights of rarified air and labored breaths . . . breaths now evened by the last drop of vodka, and the sweet ether of unconsciousness.

Somewhere between truth and illusion, where dreams live, her face and voice materialize and fade, drowned by a drumbeat pounding his senses, and he struggles against webs of sleep, yielding at last to the glycerine oblivion of not knowing.

In half-dreams a reel of film unwinds—she flees his angry critic's eye and stinging words . . . flees from insensitive response, speeds down roads that have no names, screaming, circling, turning back, letting anguish aim her car toward his forbidding gate.

Truth and dreams are intermingled in the light of day, and he stands squinting in morning sunlight, stunned by the source of night's angry sounds . . . The gate hangs starkly askew, damaged beyond repair—splintered like end punctuation she has gouged in his definition of love.

SHIRLEY COUVILLION-POWELL

The Gathering

Retreats are foreign to me, but I have come here for my friend. I want to understand what this means to all of them—to grasp how the paralysis of grief begins to heal in a place like this. I have sometimes wanted to retreat from my own pain, but I have not lost a son or a daughter, as they have. I am trying to see through their eyes, how a grief retreat with its sharing and rituals can be anything but a little bizarre. I think I am learning.

At dusk, the group drifts together near the bank of a brooding lake, anticipating the moon, eyes searching a disappearing horizon for its orange light to untangle knots of trees huddled in the gathering darkness like tall ghosts, fearful of standing alone in the night. These survivors, too, huddle in darkness, unable to discern their own shadows or their futures, unable to move on.

The world is impatient for normalcy. It does not understand the ache of loss that lingers, clinging, viscous, like a spiderweb from which no amount of motion will set the live creature free—the ache that won't let go of a beloved life cut short, lost in a collision of vulnerability with capricious fate. Here, the shuttered windows of their souls open timidly, and they are allowed their slow healing, without cloying pity or ridicule or intrusion.

Here, I can listen and not speak. Can share the remembrance of a high-spirited son piloting his small plane "The Dream Catcher," and the suddenness of all bright dreams plunging into the ocean. Begin to purge the nightmare of a three-year-old, eager for his birthday, drowning in a small creek in back of his house; remembering, instead, his astonishment at small things, his daily discoveries of the world's wonders, the exuberance and joy of his existence. Can celebrate the life, and not its brevity, of an inspired teacher, beginning to turn lights on in grade school eyes, having her own eyes dim and close from cancer so very young.

One can hear and feel the anguish of family at the death of a daughter, twenty-nine, shot and killed by her husband, as she tried to flee his abuse. Can pray for the miracle of no permanent scars on the lives of her small children, left without a mother, without a father. Can allow memory to flood with images of a boy and girl, nineteen, with stars in their eyes and the car radio playing "their" song, abruptly pictured in yearbook pose, smiling, from the rain-soaked obituaries in a morning newspaper.

Most of them want to live, want to pick up the pieces of their broken lives, want to erase death from their faces, and reaching out, to somehow help others. But the sticky web of grief still holds them, and they come here, needing help to break its grip.

The evening ritual begins, and I am uncomfortable and want to leave, but I stay—for all of them. Never one to lean on ritual, I try to have an open mind, an open heart. Try to feel what they are feeling. Even in private aloneness, a communion of spirits exists here in the solitude of trees and lake.

Each lights a candle for one life lost to this world—to its woods and lakes, its mountains and fields, its city streets. To familiar touch and scent and sound, to the sweet air and earth loves left behind. One lighted candle after another is placed on a wooden pallet, shaped and smoothed by a woodcarver grieving a loss of his own. A small canoe, dangling towrope, waits in the water, humble in its role of chariot.

And someone has penned a song about good-byes and remembrance. About love frozen in time. And the song is softly sung by the unpracticed voices in a chorus of survivors, trying to make it through one more night, one more month, one more year. Solemnly, an irrational lifeboat, heart-shaped, is placed in the still, murky waters, and the lake comes alive with the diamondshine of reflected candlelight, and the canoe

150

gently pulls its burden away from shore. Flickering lights fade in the distance, slowly becoming invisible to eyes misted again, with old tears.

As darkness crowds in, claiming oxygen from our shallow breaths, the moon rises like a benediction over this gathering of souls trying to heal. Their brief candles have burned brightly, and now drift into infinity—still shining just beyond the limited range of human vision.

KATHLEEN R. RAPHAEL

Great Blue Heron

In the fall she waits for me among the yellowing cottonwoods, standing in the straw-colored grass or wading in the brown shallows near the sandbar. I walk on the levy looking for her, *ardea herodias*. She returns when nights are cold enough to leave frost on the gravel. Both of us far south enough to spend our winters in the sun, today I do not see my old friend. Her blue-gray feathers blend with the pale patchwork of fall. Her long thin legs are no more than two slim reeds on the bank. I cannot catch the glint of the sun reflecting her dark black speck of an eye. I walk and search. I stare at the open spaces and the small groves and out over the water. Nothing. Is she fishing another bend in the river? With a rustle, the feathered tamarisk opens, and she rises on two huge, arched, flapping wings. She spans the sky, circles above the levy road and splashes into the cold river. All this time she was watching me.

CAROL J. RHODES

Vow of Silence

Even at an early age, his mother used him as a listening post. After the violent quarrels that left her in tears and his father in a bar until all hours, he would sit near her on the floor, hands clasped around his knees, and listen as she told him her problems.

From this he learned the skills of a confidant. In school he acquired the nickname of 'Father Confessor,' as fellow classmates sought both his ear and advice.

After graduation from college, he entered the priesthood and as a novice was assigned to a small parish in rural Tennessee. After taking his final vows, he replaced the older priest who had died the month before.

At first he worried because so few parishioners came to confession. But his reputation as a sympathetic listener spread, and gradually more and more came regularly to seek forgiveness.

"I ain't never been to no confession before," the man began.

"Do not be afraid in the presence of God, my son. What do you have to confess?"

"How do I know you won't tell nobody?"

"As a priest, I've taken the holy vow of silence. What you tell me here is just between you and me and God."

"Father, you see, I've done killed somebody."

"Did you have a quarrel with this person?"

"Nope. Never laid eyes on her before."

"Well then, tell me what happened. Believe me, it will help ease your pain."

So, day-by-day, little by little, details of the killing were revealed to Father Timothy.

"Last spring I was huntin' in my cousin Red's woods

when I come up on this ol' run-down shack. I was kinda curious to know who'd be livin' by theirself way out in the middle of nowhere, so I just started lookin' around. Well, I seed this ol' car sittin' under a big ol' tree . . . man, I always did want me a car like that. This one was all rusted to hell . . . but it could've been fixed up real nice. It didn't have no tires, though, even if I'd given any thought to stealin' it.

I was just standin' there admirin' it, honest, when all of a sudden this skinny ol' gray-headed woman comes tearin' around the corner of the house. She was carryin' a shotgun, an' commences orderin' me off her land like I was a criminal or somthin'. Well, I started walkin' towards her, just friendly-like, when she tells me she'll shoot if I was to come one step closer. About then's when I got real mad, raised my own gun an' fired . . . hit her smack in the middle of the chest, too . . . comes from all my target practice . . . started out as just a kid, you know. After she keeled over, her eyes was still wide open, real eerie-like, but I could tell she was stone cold dead."

"And what did you do with her body?"

"I knowed you was goin' to get to that sooner or later. I figured I'd have to do somethin' with it . . . couldn't just leave it there on the porch. So I walked around back an' finally spotted this ol' well. Probably not been used in a mightly long time, 'cause it was all overgrowed with weeds. I cleared 'em away some an' then throwed in a few rocks. When I heared 'em go *kerplunk,* I knowed there was water in it. That's when I got the idea to just cut her up. Figured it'd be easier to throw in the parts than the whole body, so I took out my huntin' knife an' went to work. Took me awhile though . . . she was one tough ol' bird, I'll tell you.

Afterwards, I had me a couple of smokes an' sat on the woman's porch awhile. The place just had a look to it like nobody was goin' to miss her 'cause I s'pect she was some kind of hermit.

Anyways, when I got back to cousin Red's place, I was carryin' three jackrabbits I'd killed an' skinned, so nobody asked me nothin' about the blood on my hands an' clothes."

Father Tim looked at his watch and remembered he'd promised to attend the parish ladies luncheon.

"My son, we'll have to talk some more tomorrow. Until then, continue to pray to God for forgiveness."

The next morning, the man was again in the confessional stall when Father Tim slid open the small door.

"Guess this'll be the last time I'll be seein' you, Father. Since I done told you everythin', there ain't nothin' much more for us to talk about, is there?" he said and slowly raised his rifle.

Transition

Dark clouds cover the horizon and the city, where large factories of dark stone sprawl and thrust their smokestacks at the sky. Out of one comes a thick column of black smoke, bent by the wind. The farther it gets from the factory, the larger it becomes. It starts to rotate, slowly at first, then faster and faster until it becomes a giant tornado into which the factory disappears.

The tornado moves down the street sucking up buildings, street lights, telephone poles, houses, stores like a huge vacuum cleaner until all traces of humanity are gone. The tornado moves into a desert where there is nothing but sand and rocks. It travels a long time.

Finally, it stops and begins to spew forth all the houses, buildings, poles in such a way that a wonderful, incredibly huge temple is constructed. When all its contents are disgorged and the temple is complete, the tornado gives one final cough and covers the entire structure with sand.

The tornado then slows its rotation and breaks up into countless little black clouds. Each cloud then rains itself away, and from every wet spot on the sand a cactus appears and bursts into iron bloom.

.38 Grief

Beside a hovering, bare-limbed oak tree, Kirk Longshadow stood in a cemetery and listened to the soft roar of early morning freeway traffic half a mile away. An hour yet until daybreak. He wondered if he had slept at all during the long night. Tossing the covers off, pulling them on again. Pacing. Staring out the window at nothing.

He shifted the weight of a .38 revolver holstered beneath his jacket and stared down at a gravestone. The letters blurred in the blue light of a mercury vapor lamp. He didn't need to read the name. He saw it every time he shut his eyes: Terry Longshadow.

If he blinked, another name emblazoned itself: Garrett Longshadow. And he dared not blink twice.

Nearby, a car coasted to a curb, radio blaring hip-hop through an open window. A chilly wind hustled a newspaper along the grass. Longshadow watched it tumble and pause, then slap against the tree trunk. A woman, bundled in layers of threadbare garments, snatched the newspaper and squinted at the headline before folding it into a tight square, which she slid into a garbage bag stuffed with aluminum cans and other refuse. Longshadow had seen the woman before, sitting beneath the same tree, sorting through odd bits in her shiny black plastic bag.

He turned away from her misery and into his own.

Was that rain? No—water striking dirt, but accompanied by the smell of urine.

"Hey, there!" the woman shouted. "Watch what you're doing over there!"

"Shad up, ol' lady." The male voice was guttural and thick with booze.

"Don't you know it's against the law to relieve yourself in public?"

"I'll take a leak anywhere I feel like it, including your pie hole if you don't shad it."

Do what he says, ma'am, Longshadow prayed wearily. But she wouldn't, of course.

The hip-hop music segued to a newscast.

"Against the law, I tell you! And the law happens to be standing right in front of us there. Hey, you! Mr. Lawman!"

Leave me alone. Longshadow refused to look.

"That ain't no cop," the man argued.

"Don't you read the newspapers?" The woman rattled her bag. "Houston cop what lost his whole family? Three in a row, fell like dominoes."

His son. His brother. His wife. Longshadow's bones felt as fragile as salt. His stomach roiled with bile.

He heard the rasp of a zipper and the shuffle of footsteps. Then the car revved and drove away.

He wiped a slick of moisture off his lip...

> *David Longshadow, nine, beloved son of*
> *Kirk and Terry, died today after a two*
> *year struggle against leukemia.*

The obituary scrolled against the inside of his closed eyelids...

> *Officer Garrett Longshadow, 32, brother*
> *of Sergeant Kirk Longshadow, was killed*
> *today in the line of duty.*

He fingered a crumpled twenty-dollar bill in his pocket...

> *Terry Longshadow, 33, eleven months*
> *after the death of her only son, died today*
> *from a sleeping-pill overdose. Terry is*
> *survived by her husband*

The .38 felt heavy against his side. Fourteen years he'd carried it, never noticing the weight. Now, it tugged at him.

He turned to the old woman and handed her the twenty.

"Please," he told her. "Don't talk about my family."

(".38 Grief" is from *Emissary*, a work in progress)

CLAIRE OTTENSTEIN-ROSS

Grandfather's Fence

Grandfather bought the farm and built the fence when he was fifty. The wood he used was from the Osage orange tree or "boise d'arc" in French. We called it "bodark." Tough and thorny, it was also used for hedges that were horse-high, pig-tight and bull strong, as grandfather used to say.

As a child, I remember him cutting down the slender tree trunks and rugged branches that would hold the gridded wire. From those came curved posts and bracing branches, irregular in size, yet lovely to the eye. I marveled at their arched limbs, and how they stretched upward toward the sky like arms raised in silent prayer. Those twisted forms proudly proclaimed their former life as growing things.

His fences protected crops, kept cattle in or out of different pastures. Sometimes I'd help him build them, hand him bowed and buckled wood. I loved to touch it, feel its hardness as my fingers ran across its roughened surface. I saw my grandfather in those sturdy tree trunks and thorny branches. He was somewhat gnarled, tall and slender too—a man of strength just like the "bodark." Those fences on his farm were his prize creation. For me they fenced in memories of joy.

JANE BUTKIN ROTH

Pushing The Button

At Alcatraz, the guards had their rules, too. Oh, yeah . . . right. What a joke. Like someone cared if the guards followed rules. We were their pets. Animals-in-a-cage. One of their rules was to leave the lights on in solitary. Right, man. Like that ever happened.

You try it. Just close your own eyes—tight. Keep them shut awhile. Don't make a noise. Pretend no one could hear you anyway. Now you think you've got it. You think you understand? You can still see light with your eyes closed. You can still dream when you've got light. But in the hole, without lights, it's nothing like closing your eyes.

It's as if your eyes have been gouged out. You're blinder than blind. The floors and walls—solid steel. No way a sliver of light's going to find its way to your sorry ass. No way you could feel one ray of hope. No way anything could ever change there. You're just lost, man. Blind. Mute. Lost.

But, even in Cell Block D, even in the hole, some days were better than some others. Those days were the first days of solitary, when I still said my prayers. When I could still think something mattered. Time mattered. I mattered. I could picture an end to it in those days. I still felt like a man.

On the best of those days, when I felt some life left in me, I'd tear a button off my coveralls. Drop it on the floor. Then I'd hunt for it in the blackness. Hunt all day for it, that one little button, so I don't feel so hunted. My button. My game. I'd search for it for hours on endless hours 'til I felt the sleek, round plastic thing. And I'll be goddamned if I didn't cry when I touched it. Cried at brushing up against something that wasn't metal or steel.

And when I finally grabbed it, I swear the damn plastic circle felt as smooth as a woman's skin I hadn't touched in

160

five years. I'd put it to my nose and I could smell my baby's perfume. Felt the button in my palm like her sweet, moist skin. I rubbed its magic into me, closed my hands around it, and just held on to it for awhile. My prize. Then I'd push it around, crawling, listening to the small, slick sound it made sliding against the cold floor. When that got old, I'd stand and drop it, start my game again.

JANE BUTKIN ROTH

Jack's Father's Hands

Jack still carried army men in his pockets and his pants didn't
fit right. His glasses kept sliding over to one side or the other
of his face, as if to constantly remind us he didn't quite match
up somehow, or there wasn't enough face for his glasses to
hold onto. He stuttered and was smaller than the rest of us
twelve-year-olds. He was different. At twelve, different is the
worst thing you can be.

Mrs. Hillard, our sixth grade teacher, treated him
differently, too. But different to her, didn't seem so bad. While
most of us were playing freeze tag or on the blacktop playing
basketball, Mrs. Hillard would talk to Jack on the playground.
She would bring him things—a magnifying glass, books,
postcards. Mrs. Hillard treated him special, and we picked on
him all the more for it. They made us feel ordinary and we, in
turn, made Jack feel weird, or even weirder than he already
was.

One day, after we spent most of lunch egging each other
on to think up something mean to do to Jack after school,
Timmy, Patrick, Jason and I agreed on how to torture Jack,
pay him back for being teacher's pet. We told him we would
meet him behind the school, that Mrs. Hillard had given us
some interesting things for him to look at under his magnifying
glass, "Y-y-yeah?" he asked, his eyes looking happy behind
his goofy glasses.

When we got him behind the school, Timmy, Patrick,
Jason and I charged him, just as he asked to see what was it
Mrs. Hillard gave us. We knocked him to the ground. Jason
put his hand over Jack's mouth, I held his arms together, and
Timmy and Patrick pulled his pants down to his ankles. It's
the first time we ever saw Jack without his glasses, which
must have flown off when we knocked him down. His face
was one big blur of confusion as I held his arms and yelled,

"J-J-J-Jack's a little s-s-sissy! J-J-J-Jack's a little s-s-sissy! N-n-n-need a magnifying glass to find l-l-little J-J-Jack! N-n-need a magnifying glass—" I was cracking myself up, rolling at my joke and at weird Jack, without glasses and half-naked. I didn't even hear Timmy, Patrick and Jason yell, "Run!"

I was surprised to find myself alone with Jack, when I felt someone grab me around my shirt collar and yank me up. I was jerked up above the ground, as if by a giant in a cartoon. I fell to the ground hard. Jack and the giant exchanged glances. He looked at Jack questioningly, and Jack nodded, stumbled to his feet, then quickly pulled up his britches. Jack's father was the biggest, tallest, scariest man I ever saw. He put his huge hands around my neck, held them there and squeezed a little, just long enough for me to see my life flash by— meaningless twelve years and all—and long enough to see my school, the other kids and the rest of the world fade away. I was alone with Jack and Jack's father's hands.

Then, Jack's father said in a deep, slow voice, "Jack has four big brothers. They were all small like Jack . . . until they turned thirteen. Just like me and Jack's uncles. The shortest of us is six-three". The lightweight is my brother Ed at two hundred and sixty pounds." He paused, took his hands off my neck, then said, "Jack's birthday's next week."

Jack's father turned to Jack, "Ready to go, Sport?"

JANET HULL RUFFIN

Swimming in Empty

It is the weave of vines circling the body of the vase that draws my attention, makes me want to wrap my hands around, press the vines into my hands. Yet twigs jut out from the neck, a shield pushing my fingers away, forcing me to look inside through the opening: a perfectly shaped O.

All I can think of now is the O of your mouth made from tubes pushed in forcing you to breathe, staying so long the O was still there in your coffin. Your body was chemo-stained mud brown, swollen, asking, asking.

I remember at the party a balloon broke loose. Your eyes followed it up. You said to me, to no one, "I don't want to fly up into the sky!" I should have said something but didn't. You were only a child but knew more about dying than I.

I sit looking into the O, swimming in empty, asking, asking. Looking for something to come in, something to fill the space, a totem, a fetish, something.

ANNETTE SCHWARTZ

Streetwalker

Her legs hung from her hips as if attached by wire and moved jerkily like a marionette. Eyes peered from dark circles. Heavily rouged lips appeared smeared. She wheezed, puffed cigarettes, filled gutters with ashes. Every Sunday she would go to church, in a stained silk dress and stockings that sagged, to pray for the baby she gave away.

Revenge

Bitter resentment grows daily. I relive times you turned over in bed and reached out to me in your need without a word of affection. Torn many times by your tongue, I also learned to wield this weapon, to pierce and wound sensitive places you try to hide. Not vindictive, I do not go for your jugular, slash no veins, cut just deep enough to leave scars and let you know how much pain is behind each one.

NAOMI STROUD SIMMONS

The New Deal, Rain and Amarillo

The whole of my childhood was divided into six parts: Amarillo, Colorado, Amarillo, Nevada, Amarillo, Roosevelt. Roosevelt? Oh yes, Roosevelt. Exactly one week after the Fourth of July in 1938, we made our way in best Sunday crepe dresses to Elmwood Park with three thousand people in this town of forty thousand. Others lined the streets from the Fort Worth and Denver Railway Station, along Polk Street, out to 24th and back down to Harrison to a platform in the park where we had worked our way to the front, as memory stores it, only a few feet from the President who smiled bare faced into a summer rain that drenched our bodies but not our enthusiasm, our hope and our spirit. He showered encouragement. He brought us rain and he would soon end our Dust Bowl. We knew it had to be true. He was bounded on the west by Washington Street and on the long stretch of blocks to the east by Harrison Street, supported by Tyler, Taylor and Polk. It had to be true. He departed, we walked taller in crepe dresses that shrunk from mid-calf to above our knees. No one complained, we only laughed with flames of new hope stoked even brighter by rain.

KATHERINE SORRELL

Market Streets

The air rings with the smell of cramped body odor, smoke, and trash. Hoards of people squeeze into the uneven stone streets of old city Jerusalem. Old men wearing long white robes, sandals, and Arab headdresses struggle to travel the crowded streets. Women veiled from head to toe in the Muslim traditional dress come with shy children hiding behind their legs. Young boys run up and down the streets with their huge green carts filled with the merchants' goods. And the merchants themselves, dressed in khaki pants and button down short-sleeve shirts man their small shops vigilantly—some chasing gullible customers with shouts and calls of "One dolla," like desperate hunters, others choosing to wait, aloof, with a deck of cards and a smoke. The customers are eager tourists who find themselves lost among the bursting shops full of spices, postcards, drums, dresses, shoes, pita bread, and valuable trinkets. They come to walk the roads that Jesus walked or pray at the Wailing Wall, but before they can even step within Jerusalem's gates, the markets are there, welcoming them into the cultural din and seizing their pocketbooks. They try to resist looking, intimidated initially by the shouting merchants, but the temptation is too great, and in only a few minutes they are bartering for market goods. In their bewilderment, they often do not realize that they are taking part in an ancient tradition that goes back to even before the Romans, back to the days when David still ruled Israel. They are shopping.

LORI ANN STEPHENS

After Five Months

They sit on the olive green couch at The Corner Cafe. They sip on three-dollar coffees and stare at cars that whiz past the storefront window. They are silent, except for the fluttering slurp of hot liquid. The cafe is almost empty. A man in a suit and tie reads a newspaper at the corner table. A woman stirs cream into her paper cup. A young man behind the counter scrubs a pot under a stream of water. The afternoon sun is already low. Trees and streets and cars and passers-by are drenched in orange-red hue, as though the world outside the cafe is dipped in henna. "How long?" she says. Her words drop like the feet of the passers-by that thud across the pavement outside. He swallows his coffee and stares at the burgundy rug beneath his feet. "I don't know. Soon, I hope." His words roll out of his mouth and fall onto the green upholstery in the space between his leg and hers. "When is soon?" she says. She doesn't look at him. She looks at the cars queued up at the stoplight. He fumbles with the wedding band, turns it around and around on his left hand. "I don't know," he says, and swallows another gulp of coffee. He looks at her. The last golden haze of afternoon fades on her face. Strands of her long dark hair reflect the red evening, and glow like a halo around her head. "I can't," she says to the cars, "It's too hard." He looks down again and studies the thin golden tassels on the Oriental rug. They are crumpled and dirty. Stepped on by thousands of coffee patrons. Lovers of coffee, lovers of caffeine. "What do you want to do?" he asks the rug. She swallows her coffee, and words wash down her throat under the flood of bitter liquid. She turns her ring with her thumb. A machine on the counter hisses and gurgles and spews froth into a cup. "What do you want?" he says. "Nights. Mornings," she says. The last sliver of sunlight casts a golden

168

glow on their skin. "I need time. Give me time. Trust me," he says. "Trust you." A muscular fist closes around the warm liquid in her stomach. She sets her cup on the table and rubs her eyebrows. "Trust you. Trust you." The fist pushes out against her lungs, pushes up into her esophagus. "Don't rush me," he says. The sun is gone, and the deepening red turns white under the fluorescent light of the cafe. "Okay," she says, and nods. "Trust you. I'll trust you." He nods and his lips curl into a half-smile. "Good," he says. He leans over and kisses her on the forehead. "I'll be home soon," he whispers. She closes her eyes and waits until she hears the squeal of couch springs. She sinks down into the olive green couch. She opens her eyes and he is outside the cafe, crosses the street and waves back at her. She lifts the cup to her lips. "Trust you," she says. She leans her head back, and cold coffee rolls down her throat. She watches the cars inch forward before the light turns green. She watches him disappear into the crowd of pedestrians on their way home, to their wives, to their husbands, to their children, to their dinners and their beds. She props her feet on the edge of the couch and tucks her knees under her chin. The man in the suit and tie shakes and folds his newspaper. "Don't trust him," he says. "Excuse me?" "He's a fool. Don't trust him," he says. She isn't angry. She isn't even curious. "He won't come back?" she asks, her cheek still resting on her knees. The man reminds her of her father, before the illness. He smiles and doesn't speak. She nods her head. He pushes the folded newspaper across the table and she stares at the cars whizzing by. The black night unfolds over the neon signs and the yellow lamplight.

CHUCK TAYLOR

Southern Man

She called wanting money, I told her no more, I'd heard from his mom what she and he were spending it on, I didn't know why and I didn't care, they should stop.

I'd be by the next day early afternoon, I told her, with sacks of groceries because he's my son and works long hours down at the Ice House being the kitchen manager and I knew she'd be home—and how were they doing, I hadn't seen her or Billy in a long shot, not the four months since he left the joint where I used to stare at him through thick glass, and I asked why she quit her job, what's the use staying at home when you ain't got no kids.

And I went by in the cold November rain the next day, lugging the groceries up the stairs to the door, wanting to see what's up cause she'd always been a looker, nice, though she was mad at her dad's drinking, 'What do you expect from a southern man?'—she'd often told me, and she cut the door and stared out from the darkness inside, I could see she wasn't dying her hair no more, I could see the pimples on her face, her gray nightgown she didn't bother to hold closed.

And I said can I come in and she stepped away from the door and I tried to find a place to set down the bags but the table and counter were covered with unwashed plates and Styrofoam cups with black dredges of coffee inside and there were piles of books stacked around the bed from the Houston library, mostly novels and books on feminism—she was smart, Jamie, though she never finished school, so I turned around in that efficiency a few times, cigarette butts smashed on the kitchen floor and Dorito chips lying around, and set the groceries on the floor next to the door.

And then I heard the toilette flush and thought my son was home early or taking the day off, but out came Rhone I'd known since my boy was fourteen and they had a band, their

170

equipment taking up the basement and my tools disappearing and the neighbors calling to ask if they would turn it down.

Rhone, tall and skinny like before he'd gone to prison because he'd found his girlfriend in bed with her ex, and in the parking lot outside the duplex off Hempstead, they'd quarreled and then shot each other, and the ex died on the way to the hospital, but the girlfriend said Rhone shot in self-defense.

Now I am a security guard since Dell let me go and the wife moved up north to be with her mother, I got a permit to carry a gun and I wasn't in uniform but I had on my raincoat and a Sig 226 holstered inside under the left arm and I put my hand inside the coat like the pictures of Napoleon, but I could see the boy's right hand reaching up across to his left sleeve where his Camels were rolled up, and he said, Mr. Sanders, good to see you, I just got here myself, your son Bill asked me to take Jamie, she's going to apply to be a school bus driver.

And I said, that's great Jamie you like kids that's great and nodded and I turned my back and sweating, kneeled, picked off the floor the groceries, and I went out the door, down the slippery steps in the cold and rain.

CAROL KINCHELOE TESCH

Club Drama

The sign just outside the door read, "DRINK MORE BEER. WHAT DOES NOT KILL YOU ONLY MAKES YOU STRONGER."

My friend Matt and I entered the club about eight, primetime for comfortable talk with the savvy-minded bartender. He shoved a Coors-Lite my way. (Experience smells inexperience.) Other customers were jovial, connecting. The air was fresh. Tables were clean and glasses sparkled. Two musicians occasionally plucked out crude sounds to disturb the stillness. Beer signs illuminated aged pool tables.

We chose a corner table and chatted about problems, the ones you create and the others that create you. I like to listen to Matt's problems. They all center around female feelings and physiology. Anyway, the telling of his problematic love life wasn't such a downer that he didn't notice the dominatrix-type (his words) in the black-lace camisole standing about five feet in front of our table. The intimate quietness dissipated when the first rowdy group tromped in about nine-thirty. The atmosphere exploded quickly.

A burly white guy announced our singer for the night, "Miss Pearl." The fifty-something soul "diva" took the platform and ate up the mike. After a few brassy tunes my friend shook his head and complained, "These guys are lousy, there's no feel."

I grinned, "Hey just put a little right brain into it. Let that bass guy do his stuff and you fill in the rest." Pearl belted out *Proud Mary*. We zigzagged through a wall of people to claim our turf on the miniscule dance floor. Bodies bounced in free radical expression. Athletic shoes, blue jeans, and suits all vied for the same space. Sweat and perfume are a curious mix.

Between songs Matt tried to educate me on the necessity of a woman speaking like a man, being humorous, revealing true feelings, using strong nouns. He explained how males schmooze the opposite sex and women b.s. back. "A man likes a confident woman."

I answered, "Okay, let me get this. I should be straightforward, no games, keep my adjectives to a minimum, don't use bigger words than you can understand, stick to concrete details, tell dirty jokes and bare my soul, naked?" It was Matt's turn to grin. "You got it."

The air grew smokey and thick. Short-term gratification fueled the place. People milled. Women stroked egos and guys fondled their beer bottles. They also grabbed their women's rears. (Hard to say which they took more pleasure in, action or reaction.) Pearl took her break. I danced in my seat and Matt sipped down black Guiness. "What a beer," Matt proudly exclaimed as if he had helped in the actual brewing. I downed a mouthful. (Rocket fuel, elephant breath, what else can I say.) The band's last intermission concluded and Matt and I walked outside. Neons, fluorescents, and humidity-loving kissing bugs greeted us. I breezily announced, "I'll call you next week."

Matt placed his arm around me and whispered something aggressive and male. I replied, "Matt, you took chemistry, right? Remember all those boring terms like bonding, energy, explosion, physical changes."

"Yeah."

"Well, it ain't going to happen." *And that's as man as I get.*

JACK L. THOMAS

Release

I wade into the rivulet. I spread, lower my arms and immerse my hands in the water. I splay my fingers. The water, unimpeded, chortles . . . wraps around my body and hurtles forward.

I eye the mountain slope. Oak, hickory, and maple, awash in flame, secrete reds and oranges and yellows amidst an emerald sea of pine.

I climb an outcrop. A capricious wind blows the scent of burning hickory. I too burn, more in fury than passion, unsure of the hidden spring from which it soars.

I reach for words full of heft that droop and sag and do not fit, then drift away. I drop to my knees and ask, please God, fill my soul. A passel of words gushes forth, takes shape. With hands outstretched, I run for them . . . and leap.

JACK L. THOMAS

Dust

A small creek rippled alongside. Snow melt, mostly. The road tracked the stream. I downshifted into third, clipped a smooth line through the turn and accelerated out of the curve. A straightaway, perhaps a half-mile in length, ran before me. I looked up. A hawk circled above, its nose tipped down in mock judgment, amused by my attempt to emulate free flight.

As I descended the pass, the conifers gave way to aspen; the aspen thinned to poplars—black cottonwoods whose broad leaves blotted the sky. Abruptly, the mountains peeled away like jet fighters, and the broad Montana sky unfurled, bathing the township in sapphire muslin. The narrow creek probed the outskirts, then crept cautiously through the town and spread its fern-lined banks like a peacock fans his tail.

I pulled into the service stop and dismounted.

"What's that?" she said.

I cocked my head in her direction. She lay there, sunning. A weathered, barn-wood home claimed space next door.

"A motorcycle," I said.

She had stood up by now. Dust from the parched lawn swirled about her feet, coloring them dusty-gray.

"I know, silly. I mean what kind?"

"A BMW."

"Smooth."

"Like silk."

I gassed up, then went inside and paid. When I came back out, she had resumed her position on the chaise lounge. She put her arms behind her neck and stretched. Her breasts arched round and graceful like a strung recurved bow.

"Do you ride through here often?" she said.

"Not often enough."

"I miss the water so, and the growing season is short.

My tan lines. . . ."

She left the sentence for me to complete—her lines, sharp and shapely, protective barriers to her sacredness.

"I want to live in the sun," she said.

"Susan!" came the male voice from inside.

She rose, walked dutifully towards the house.

By the time she returned, I had donned my helmet and was ready to push the starter button.

"The growing season is short," she said.

I nodded.

MARK THONSSEN

Prisoner

The small cabin was dark and stale. He lay on the hard cot, a bare wooden frame topped with dirty straw and some old rags. The single lantern swayed from its hanger overhead as the ship, creaking and groaning with every new wave, lurched upon the sea. He'd become used to the movement. At first, he'd been dreadfully ill, weak and starved from lack of nourishment, for nothing he ate would remain long in his stomach. The stains of vomit that splattered across the wooden planks of the far corner were dry now, their acrid odor gone, the stains fading into the woodwork. He was stronger now, though still weak. The three meals served him each day were bland and monotonous, but nourishing.

A series of notches in the woodgrain above the cot had once marked the days. Such things no longer mattered; one day seemed lost among so many others just like it.

The Captain had allowed him books, occasionally, and sometimes fresh paper, ink and a quill. A journal was pointless when he could no longer tell the days from one another, and with no portholes nor slits in the walls of his cabin, he had no idea where he was. He'd written a request to the Captain, long ago, asking for a period of time on deck, for fresh air and exercise, a chance to gaze at clouds and sky and sea again. Nothing had come of it. He'd written several more times with the same results.

They would not, of course, deliver any message ashore for him; the war kept the ship at sea for much of the time, and ports of call were brief and in friendly waters—friendly for the ship and its crew, at least. Not for him.

A knock at the door stirred him from his thoughts.

"Who is it?"

"Lieutenant Allain, sir." The lock clicked and the door opened. The lieutenant poked his head into the cabin. "The

Captain has granted your request."

He sat up quickly. "I'm to be allowed topside?"

"Yes, sir, with an escort. If you'll come with me."

Allain led him from the cabin; another officer, also carrying a pistol at his side, followed close behind.

After so long in the lantern's twilight, the sheer intensity of the sunshine hurt his eyes. The two officers helped him ascend the stairway to the open deck. The sight of blue sky was enough to make his knees tremble. He could not remember the last time he had been in open air.

It was a beautiful day. Few clouds dotted the serene blue sky, its bright reflection made the ocean seem but part of it. A light wind crossed the deck, the sails snapping as the ship rolled gently back and forth. Standing at the railing, he pulled in great lungs of sea air, fresh and cool, tasting of salt and summer rain. Below decks, the odor of the sea was old and stale, like low tide mixed with tar and sweat and gunpowder. On deck, he could not breathe enough of it.

On shaky legs he worked his way along the railing. Rounding the stern, he was startled to see a coastline near.

Land!

He hadn't realized the ship was so close to shore, a few miles at most from the judge of it. How long had it been since he'd stood on solid ground? He didn't remember.

Holding the rail tightly, he gazed longingly at the coastline. In a way, it reminded him of home—the white rock shores, the slender cypress trees in a line like soldiers marching over the hills, the stone lighthouse on the outcropping of land. . . .

It *was* home. His first instinct was to leap over the rail into the sea, and swim ashore. In his present health, he knew he would as likely drown before reaching shore. *But, oh, to try!*

The metallic click behind him told him the lieutenant had cocked the hammer on his pistol, no doubt to prevent him from doing just that. With a sinking feeling, he realized he'd be dead before he hit the water.

He stood gripping the wooden railing, the ship shifting on the waves, and watched his homeland drift slowly astern, so close, so far away.

He watched a long time, till the land was no more than a slim shadow that lay upon the horizon. His face was wet, the breeze cold on his skin. The salt of the sea now tasted bitter, and his stomach suddenly felt like it had at the beginning of the voyage, so long ago.

A cold emptiness twisted in his gut, and he felt weary beyond measure.

"Take me below," he said.

CAROLYN TOURNEY

Immigrants

Thilakasiri, the husband, was the first to say, "We must go!" She was in shock. Thamara, the wife, still did not believe that such a miracle could happen to her, to her family. Out of all the tens of millions of people, the millions of families, hers was the one chosen by God, she believed, to depart their homeland, Sri Lanka, to immigrate to the United States of America.

It is hot and Tharindu, the twelve-year-old son, is on his way to school. He walks under the sun, the same sun children all over the world walk under. Tharindu travels almost a mile to catch a bus that will take him to his school in Colombo, the largest city in Sri Lanka. He adjusts his glasses on his thin face. He looks gaunt, his large dark eyes deeply placed in his face. His worn and ill-fitting clothes, pull tightly on his thin body. This year he has grown so quickly that he is taller than his father. Tharindu has been taller than his mother for two years.

School is serious. There is no time for idle conversation with friends. Tharindu is late this morning. He enters through the doorway and filters in as quietly as does the sunlight. The teacher does not notice him, or perhaps, pretends not to notice. The day melts away for Tharindu because he loves his studies, absorbing unquestionably all his lessons.

There is a tattered pigeon limping near the bus stop. As Thilakasiri, the father, waits for his bus that will take him to his teaching job at the technical institute, he watches the pitiful bird. One reddish leg has only a melted stub for its foot. It hobbles, then falls onto its chest, bare of feathers, pushed off balance by a whirl of other pigeons scrambling for spilled rice. There is a small pain in Thilakasiri's heart as he watches the bird. He enters the overcrowded bus and stands pressed against the front windows. A shimmer of pigeons uplift before his eyes. The crippled bird lurches for the left-over grains. Thilakasiri smiles. So that is how the bird lives!

Thamara is at her work. She sits before a computer, an outdated one by most standards. Each day she enters data, many thousands of grains of information she stores away. Thamara is thankful to have her job, a husband and a son. She is thankful for her home, an apartment where they all live together near her parents. She doesn't think often of places beyond Sri Lanka, but Thamara is aware that such places like Europe, Great Britain, Australia and the USA exist. She knows her geography. When her lottery number is picked out of millions of others, when she finds out that she and her family have been granted a green card to the U.S., she searches her apartment for her atlas to find out exactly where Houston, Texas is located. It is so much further north than Sri Lanka and halfway around the world. She can hardly believe that it exists. It is beyond her imagination.

Thilakasiri and his family use all their savings to transport them to Texas. Furniture is sold, even clothes. All they leave behind is an invisible hope that life will be better in America and they will call back for the others in their family to join them.

"God has brought us here!" Thilakasiri declares as they step off the plane. It is all so marvelous and exotic. People of all colors, rushing people, fill the airport terminal. People speaking English and Spanish and tongues unrecognizable to them. People looking as amazed and lost as Thilakasiri and his family.

On the curbside they wait for a bus to take them away from the airport and into the city. Beside them is their luggage containing their only possessions. They stand so close to each other there is no space for the sunlight to come between their bodies. Together they feel the blast of heat, the hot embrace of Texas air. For a moment they feel an ease, a fading of disbelief and fear. For a moment they feel this new place could be home.

MARK TWEEDY

Sir

"You're not going to believe this but. . . ."

That was it. The commander never said another word. We avoided each other's eyes, more embarrassed than anything else. When the train slowed to a limp, they rolled his body out of the boxcar, then stood at attention as what had once been our leader disappeared down the embankment. He flopped and twisted his way to the waterline in an otherwise comical gravity dance. It wasn't that interesting and they soon returned to their places in the filth. All our movements had faded to tropisms by then.

What could the old man have meant? I sat looking backwards, watching dark hills unfurl in the world we had left. What was it that could we not believe? We who had seen such creative butchery that all the demons of Hell could only stand by in mute awe and take notes. The war had merely been a testament to our own necrotic imagination.

What could we not now believe? I pulled more smoke into my lungs and nearly fell asleep. Each time I nodded off I saw the girl I had loved. I say "loved" not because I've stopped but because the situation became untenable.

She hadn't minded that I was the enemy. From the moment I saw her, arbitrary borders were the furthest things from my mind. Of course we never actually met the entire time we were together. She loved a man in uniform and I loved being out of it. Even now her furtive eyes peek through a wisp of blonde hair just out of my reach.

We lived without names for what could have been months. She could just puzzle out my language but I never found my way through hers. We healed the wounds of our nations in our bed each night. Not that we knew it at the time.

We were too strong for symbolism then; and too much ourselves.

This is what matters. When I told her I was leaving, she handled it as though she had knocked a glass to the floor— quietly and efficiently. The crucible we'd made had boiled away any cloying personal details, leaving a pure and untouchable memory. It left us not empty but in the quiet of a concert hall with the orchestra's last lingering note.

I lit another cigarette on a smoldering filter. What kind of damn fool was this commander who couldn't even finish his last sentence? He wasted the remnants of his breath telling us we wouldn't believe what he didn't have time to tell us? Why not share that pearl of wisdom and let us decide its credibility?

The train whined its way onto a spidery trestle bridge, now high above the river. A hypnotic ostinato of grinding metal played out the theme of our final day together. She conducted herself with the appropriate sadness. We pronounced the required lines. The day never came to an end but only stopped. A picnic on wet cement in the ruined city, the sun warming her hair, the promise not to miss each other and the night settled over us in its awkward way.

In the last moments before an explosion ripped through the train, shattering the trestle and bringing us crashing down into the river far below—the same river that temporarily held our commander upstream—only in those last moments I came to understand what he had meant. We would never believe that we would be becoming him.

We who had come to regard each other with such contempt were no more than scattered reflections of the same life. It is fear of what we share that drives us to create our histories. The illusion of identity, the myth of fingerprints— the warmth of it overwhelmed me. If we all live the same life then birth and death are details. Our screams and cries are frights in a fun house.

In that last moment I could hear every conversation, every last word. Each syllable pounded out the desperate attempts at classification, at selfness. As though volume alone could separate us one from the other, denying the only gift we have. I wanted to shout back to them but there was no more I and there was no more time. And they wouldn't believe.

Denial in the face of the inevitable is absurd. The only reasonable response to the absurd is laughter. I and what could no longer be called I laughed. In disdain, in sympathy, in surprise, I laughed until the roar of the dynamite drowned out these their last words.

"Which is . . .

"What I started to say . . .

"In the first place. . . ."

BEV VINCENT

Ghost Ship

Edward looked out over the cold bay, its surface illuminated by the diffuse light of the full moon radiating through a dense fog. He wondered what it would be like to slip beneath the glimmering surface and vanish. Yield to the sirens' call and move on to whatever came next.

In the distance, the phantom ship burned furiously, the crackling of her timbers echoing in his ears.

"It's true that I love someone else, but I'm not leaving you for him," Maria had said. "I still love you, but you deserve better than me. I should be by myself."

The phantom ship, some said, was the specter of a French galleon from an historic battle. Others insisted it was nothing more than an optical illusion. Whatever the explanation, tonight the masts burned brighter than ever. Officers worked furiously to save their dying ship. Crewmen leapt from bow and stern into unforgiving waters.

Edward knew that relationships could disintegrate over time, but hadn't realized they could collapse overnight. That some cataclysm could sink a marriage in such a short period left him stunned.

Breathless.

Tears would not be held back. His body shook uncontrollably as sobs of despair escaped him.

She still loved him, but she also loved somebody else. Could he not understand that?

"I don't want this to be the end for us," he had responded.

She had been gone for two days. No matter how much he wanted their relationship to survive, it was beyond his control.

Flame-lit smoke danced in front of the moon. The phantom ship was miles offshore but voices carried across the surface. He heard panic and disbelief. Orders shouted and

185

ignored. More crew members threw themselves into the bay and vanished from sight.

Edward couldn't imagine what life was going to be like without Maria beside him when he woke up in the morning. Despair washed over him, drowning his spirits. He stared through the flames until their edges lost focus.

Random thoughts ricocheted through his mind. He could not fathom the process of separating. Untangling two intimately intertwined lives. The practicalities of financial dissolution. The impossibility of emotional resolution.

The fog grew thicker, making it difficult to discern the ship's features. One towering mast collapsed in a shower of sparks. Edward imagined the trapped crewmen struggling to extricate themselves as the flames descended.

He was aware of her standing behind him before she spoke. "I was stupid," she said. "Can you forgive me?"

Tears streamed down Edward's face. His heart beat so furiously he thought his chest would explode. He turned toward her, his answer plain on his face.

The fire was mostly extinguished. Hot spots smoldered but were under control. Crewmen clambered out of the bay, up rope ladders lowered by the officers.

Listing slightly to starboard, wounded but not lost, the phantom ship sailed into the fog and vanished.

SUE VOLK

Senior Prom

I awake to the songs of the many birds that migrate through Texas every April. Ecstatic, I suppose, that they're halfway home from their southern retreat in Guatemala. I stretch and luxuriate in the crisp ironed sheets, watching the orange sunlight creep in through the closed blinds.

"Good morning," floats my sister Elizabeth's sleepy voice from across the room. I push up on one elbow and look into her sapphire eyes, her most memorable asset. I hate myself that I have always been jealous of them.

"Have you forgotten?" she asks. "Tonight's the big dance."

"Oh, I had for a minute. I was just listening to the amazing variety of birds. I'm so glad Daddy taught us about them." I lie back once again and smile to myself. How we've looked forward to this day! It seemed it would never come. But here it is before us, looming with all kinds of potential. I shudder in anticipation. "It'll be wonderful. I wonder if everyone will be there." *If John will be there.* My heart flutters erratically at the thought of his twinkly eyes, contagious smile.

"Mama helped me pick out the most beautiful dress," Elizabeth says. "Pale blue silk with tiny white flowers embroidered on the bodice. Fits me like a dream. I wonder what shoes to wear. Should bag and shoes match?"

"It's more interesting if they don't."

"Good, because I don't want to worry about it."

I sit up in bed and look over at her. "I'm getting a manicure today. Want me to make you an appointment?"

"Oh, that would be lovely," she murmurs. She pats her thin fine hair. "Maybe I'll get my hair done too. It's just not behaving lately. What are you wearing tonight?"

I pick up the hand mirror on the bedside table and look into it. Piercing hazel eyes stare back and I smile, thinking

187

they are exactly like Daddy's. I'd always been his favorite. A tomboy, ready to run and jump, fish and play ball. The son he never had.

"I'm wearing that yellow dress that brings out the gold flecks in my eyes. It makes me feel happy, and Daddy always said yellow's my best color."

A sniff. "Well, Daddy likes me in blue. But does that dress still fit? You've lost some weight."

"It'll be all right. Only you would notice."

Unexpectedly the door flies open, startling us in our reveries.

"Time to get up, sleepyheads. Breakfast is being served in the dining room. Are you ready for the big dance? It's going to be a lively one."

I squint as the interloper opens the blinds and the dazzling sunlight pours in. She turns to prop open the door.

"Mama," Elizabeth murmurs and raises her arms. Then Nurse Laurie gathers my octogenarian sister in her arms, gently arranges her in the wheelchair, and pushes it toward the door. I reach for my walker and slowly make my way behind her.

The nurse looks back and smiles. "This is going to be the best dance Sunset Manor ever had."

LEONA WELCH

Desert's Song

Thin finger rocks rise in the distance—pale painted shadows chase sand devils across dry lakes and desert dunes. Vast barren plains, harbor of refuge for outcasts seeking shade from the burning sun. Creatures of slithering grace hide in barren pockets. Crawling death abounds with spiders and scorpions. Vultures on wing give truth of hazards beyond a point of no return. Sun devils dance on winds from hell, racing through arroyos. Coyotes sing songs; mournful sounds beyond reality. Cactus needlepoints stretch toward the sun, keeping others to distance for safety's sake. Blooms of Octillio, bring beauty to this forsaken kingdom with fields of blazing orange. Beyond raised arms of century aged saguaro, the sun slips behind royal purple hues; vague, veiled gloom makes distance deceiving. Between these desert borders devils live in harmony with sand and sun; no patience with intruders who come on man-made machines. Beyond caring! Digging! Slashing! Leave waste in their path! Marked souvenirs in their wake complete the destruction of desert sands. Spinning devil wheels sing new songs, and man treks new land searching realms to conquer all within his view. Barren beauty and death; work of devils completely deaf to songs of the sun.

GERALD R. WHEELER

Windy's New Course

Windy stepped into the van, choked on formaldehyde fumes, saw jars, traps and supplies, felt a tingle in her spine. Ten hours later, on a trail in Big Bend, she pointed at a coiled snake and asked, "Is that a black-tailed rattlesnake, Dr. Lee?" The teacher nodded, told her to fetch the potato-hook. When Windy returned, all she saw were squiggles in the sand. Dr. Lee pointed to the bulge in a gunnysack. "Your snake, Windy," he assured, instructing her to retrieve a chloral hydrate syringe. She quivered at the thought of holding the lethal creature down and stabbing its elongated heart. But a kind classmate came to her rescue, dropped the specimen in a preservation jar. Hands pressed in prayer, she said, "Thankya, Lawrrd." By noon, she was chased into a prickly pear cactus by a collared lizard, and nearly shot her professor with a blowgun aimed at a Kangaroo rat that would not surrender. Worried over not making her quota, she broke her nails setting traps and was attacked by fire ants. At dawn, Windy checked the traps. That's when peeling varmint skin and hanging decapitated heads in flesh-eating beetle cages began. She grimaced. "It smells like a slaughterhouse here."

Four hours later, she reached into her purse for change for a coke at a gas stop, and pulled out a green snake. "That's it!" she shouted, and then made an emergency call to the University of Texas. "Dean, this is Windy Avery. I'm changing my major to English Lit."

LOUNELL WHITAKER

The Dream Catchers

Deep in reminiscent thought, he brushes the dust from his Baldwin piano and the sixty-year dream Mary tossed him when she was ten and he was three. It was her dream, then. She was the one who stretched her small hands across the keyboard, while he sat on the floor, legs pretzeled beneath him, neck craned toward her instrument, mind agape at the wonder of its sound. Every day the ritual was the same: she, dutifully practicing scales; he, sitting spellbound at her feet . . . until that day she scooped him up and taught him to play "Hot Cross Buns" with one finger on three black keys.

He began formal piano lessons on his sixth birthday, and by the time he was nine, he frolicked easily through passages Mary found impossible to play.

But the contents of his home tell the story best: from the stacks of music piled high on a closet shelf, the army of trophies proudly displayed in a curio cabinet, the black framed "Master of Music" degree and certificates of merit lining half a bedroom wall . . . to his bureau drawers stuffed full with unpublished compositions.

Tenderly, almost reverently, he opens up the keyboard and plays a selection from Mozart. He knows the piece by heart— where each crescendo begins, where it ends, which notes to accent, which notes to hold. . . . Suddenly, he glances at his watch, rises quickly from his backless bench and rushes out the door. He must not be late again for his job at the store. Turning the key in the ignition, he ponders the hours spent, the sacrifices made for music's sake, and then he smiles. The other day, he taught a young grandson to play "Hot Cross Buns" with one finger on three black keys.

191

CYNTHIA WIER

Tap Root

We are a family of broken boughs, split branches protruding across a forest of torn dreams, false starts. We crawl away from the mother trunk only to return for its healing sap.

Some of our limbs stand tall, grow broader before reaching out to fashion our own jagged leaves. Others creep slowly out in frail sprouts under the bower of shade, spindly twigs aching for the balm of sun and rain.

We are a whole tree, often parched and dry, crying for love, but strong.

CYNTHIA WIER

Wednesdays

Early morning, nightgown flowing, broom in one hand, she darts from table to sink to pantry trash can, sweeping, dusting, washing, quickly drying cups, plates, piling forks, spoons and bowls into the dishwasher, a handy storehouse for her stained utensils.

After all it's Wednesday, and she goes into overdrive to collect her stash of bills, invitations, newsletters stacked by the kitchen phone. Dumping coffee grounds into the trash, she glances around, sighs with approval, grabs a sip of Diet Coke on her way up the stairs.

Again dismayed, she scans the unsightly bedroom scene where shoes, unmatched, dot the carpet, his shirt and pants, her skirt, jacket, and scarf are thrown over the faded chintz club chair in the corner by the window, and more dishes clutter the night stand. Eyeing the time on the clock radio, she begins to strip the bed, throws sheets, blankets and pillowcases out into the hallway, and reaches for socks and underwear strewn on the floor by the bed.

On the small round table by the lamp, she starts to pick up a wine glass, half empty, by the two vanilla votives, melted almost to the bottom, and red and silver foil wraps from the chocolate kisses, memories of last night. She stops, walks to the window and smiles.

Slowly moving into the bathroom, she strips, draws a hot bath, and locks the door. The maid has her own key to the house.

Aunt Dora's Box

Dear LaVerle,

I survived registration, an event that resembles a stampede on the Salt Grass Trail, and my first week at State U. Don't tell my folks, but I've wished I was back in Bingham at least a thousand times. I didn't know a soul when I first arrived, and sitting by myself in the cafeteria was so awful that I skipped three meals. My roommate arrived on the third day of Freshmen Orientation and saved me from starvation.

I can't wait for the two of you to meet. I've told her all about you—well, almost all. Her name is Judy Edmonds, and she's from a place called Marble Falls. She's got a wonderful sense of humor, but the best thing about her is her size. Remember how I worried about getting a doll-sized roommate who would make me feel like a cow? Well, Judy is 5'11" tall and wears a size ten shoe.

My classes are pretty interesting. Judy says I'm lucky to be enrolled in honors, because we get the best teachers, but I have my doubts about Professor Blake. He's my honors philosophy professor. On the first day of class, he made all the students stand up and tell something about themselves— where they went to school, what they planned to do, stuff like that. When my turn came I remembered Papa Bradley's instructions to stand tall and be proud of who I was. With my shoulders back and my chin high, I said, "I'm Beth Bradley, and I'm from Bingham, Texas." Then I sat down. Most people told more about themselves than that, but I couldn't think of anything else. I thought about saying I was head drum majorette of the Bingham High School Band, but the counselor at Freshmen Orientation told us we'd get along better at State U if we put all that high school stuff behind us. Besides, I'm not head drum majorette anymore. Gloria Sims is now. It's a good thing I sat down, before I made a fool out of myself.

Then Professor Blake gave an hour lecture on "The State of Being." All I got out of it was that none of us can be sure whether or not we exist. I'm trying to keep an open mind like that counselor at Freshmen Orientation told us to do, but all the time Professor Blake was talking, I was thinking that the only other person I've known who wasn't sure he existed was Mr. Doyle. You remember Mr. Doyle. When our Girl Scout Troop went to the State Home to sing Christmas carols, Mr. Doyle was the old man who kept pinching our bottoms to see if we were alive or dead like him.

Judy's brother had Professor Blake for philosophy last year, and Judy says her brother swears that Professor Blake is smart, has two Ph.D.'s behind his name and has written a bunch of books. Maybe so, but I still think someone who isn't sure he exists needs to see a doctor.

So far, Psychology 101 makes a lot more sense than Philosophy 132. We've been talking about heredity and environment, and which one is more important. My psychology prof said environment—time, locale, and culture—is as important as heredity. I disagreed at first, until she explained that our families are both heredity and environment. Our term assignment is to keep a memory notebook and write in it every day of the fall semester. The prof says names and dates aren't important. We are to be more concerned with impressions that people and events have made on our memories than with historical accuracy. She says if we write in our memory books every day we should have a better understanding of who we are and why we are who we are by the end of the semester.

I started writing in mine tonight. I had only written a couple of sentences when I thought about that myth Papa Bradley used to read to us. You remember, the one about the girl and boy who opened Aunt Dora's Box and got more than they bargained for.

Our dorm checker just stuck her head in the door and announced lights out. I have to sign off. Write back soon and tell me everything that's been going on in Bingham. Have you met any cute boys at BJC yet?

Hugs and kisses,
Beth

P.S. I almost forgot—My psychology prof said we could include letters in our memory books. If you don't mind, I'm going to include this letter to you. Don't worry. No one but my psychology prof is ever going to read it.

Contributors' Notes

Contributors' Notes

V.T. ABERCROMBIE (Houston): Her poems have appeared in literary magazines such as *Roanoke Review, White Rock Review, Bluegrass Literary Review, Rising Star, Slant, Madison Review, Pudding, Raintown Review, Pleiades, American Poets & Poetry, Borderlands, Illya's Honey, Visions International,* several anthologies and a recent chapbook, *V.T. Abercrombie, Greatest Hits, 1980-2000,* put out by Pudding House Publishers, Co-Editor *Christmas in Texas,* Co-Author *Catering in Houston, Places to Take a Crowd in Houston,* author of *Houston Party File.*

KAYE VOIGT ABIKHALED (Austin): She was born in Berlin, attended high school in the U.S. as a scholarship winner and immigrated in 1960. She has published in state, national and international journals and on the internet. A finalist in the 1998 Faulkner Creative Writing Competition for poetry, she edits *A Galaxy of Verse,* was appointed Councilor for the Poetry Society of Texas and chosen as a Hilton Ross Greer Outstanding Service finalist. She attended the Paris American Academy and is a recent finalist of the 2000 Fernando Rielo Mystical Poetry Prize in Madrid, the first distinction of a manuscript submitted in English in the Foundation's twenty-year history.

ANN K. ANDERSON (Conroe): Ann is a former newspaper and magazine writer turned fiction writer. She has recently added ghost writing to her list of skills which includes editing both fiction and nonfiction. Her short stories have appeared in *Amelia Magazine* and *Suddenly III.*

GEORGE AYRES (Austin): He writes screenplays and has had two one-act plays performed in New York, as well as a staged reading of a full-length play in Austin. Among others, he has been published in the *Houston Chronicle, New York Press, Santa Fe Chronicle, Street News (NY,NY), Pitchfork, Blue Review* (online), and *Passenger* (forthcoming online).

WENDY BARKER (San Antonio): She is professor of English at The University of Texas at San Antonio. Her fourth collection of poetry, *Way of Whiteness* (Wings Press, 2000) won the Violet Crown Book Award and was placed on the recommended reading list of the NBCC. Forthcoming are: poetry in *Poetry, Kenyon Review, Partisan Review*, and *New York Quarterly*; a collection of translations from the Bengali of Rabindranath Tagore (with Saranindranath Tagore) from George Braziller, Inc., Publishers; poems and accompanying essays from Absey & Company. Wendy spent the fall as a Fulbright Professor in Bulgaria.

WILLIAM McCARGO BARNES (The Woodlands): He is a retired geologist who has been writing for about three years. He has received honorable mentions for a mainstream novel and two short stories in the Woodlands Writers Guild 2000 conference. As a member of the Panhandle Professional Writers Guild in Amarillo, and will have a short fiction piece appear in their 2001 anthology. An essay appeared in the "State Lines" section of "Texas Magazine" published by the *Houston Chronicle*.

D. CREASON BARTLETT (Dallas): He grew up in Southeast Texas, attended Lamar University in Beaumont where he received a B.A. and M.A. in literature and creative writing. He is currently a Ph.D. candidate at The University of Texas at Dallas.

NANCY BERTONCELJ (Angleton): She studied under John Gorman, Professor of English and Creative Writing at the University of Houston at Clear Lake. Her work has appeared in *Cats, Image Magazine, Sulphur River Literary Review* and other publications.

IRENE BOND (Houston): She has published in *Texas Magazine*, the *Houston Chronicle, Guideposts*, short story anthologies and periodicals, and is currently finishing a mystery novel.

SHARON ECKERT-BOSWELL (Houston): Sharon writes poetry and fiction. *Visions,* a collection of her poetry, has been recorded on audiocassette. She has published two books and is working on a legal thriller.

ANN REISFELD BOUTTE (Houston): She has been a feature writer for a daily newspaper and national wire service. She is now concentrating on essays, features and poetry. Her work has appeared in the *Houston Chronicle, My Table, Lilliput Review, Texas Poetry Calendar 2000* and *2001* and other publications.

ROBERTA PIPES BOWMAN (Fort Worth): She is the author of eight books of poetry including one selected for the 1995 Lucidity Chapbook Award, and is 1998 Hilton Ross Greer Award recipient from the Poetry Society of Texas. Recent publications include *Descant* (TCU), *New Texas 2000, Galaxy of Verse, Lucidity, SOL Ezine*.

MICHAEL BRACKEN (Waco): He is the author of *Bad Girls, Deadly Campaign, Even Roses Bleed, In the Town of Dreams Unborn and Memories Dying, Just in Time for Love, Psi Cops, Tequila Sunrise* and more than 700 shorter works published in commercial and small press publications. He lives in Waco with his family.

MARTHA EVERHART BRANIFF (Houston): Her novel *Beds of Broken Glass* was a finalist in the Bellwether Prize and was also a winner in the 2000 Houston Writers' League Contest. Her poetry and prose poems have appeared in *2000 Texas Poetry Calendar, New Texas 2000, A Writers Choice: Literary Journal* and will be in *My Kitchen Table* in 2001. A short story and a painting appeared in *WIVLA* 2000 Anthology.

ELIZABETH BRATTEN (Houston): She is a new writer who has studied with Christopher Woods at The Women's Institute.

ARLENE WHITE-BRISCO (Houston): She is a native Houstonian with a BS in Chemistry from Texas Southern University and a MBA from the University of Houston. Before she resigned two years ago to become a full-time mother, she was a management consultant for nonprofits. This is her first published work.

JEANNETTE BROWN (Knoxville, TN): She grew up in East and North Texas; Austin was her home for thirty years. She earned a Master's Degree in Urban Studies, but has worked in publicity for theatre, dance and other art groups. Her writing has appeared in the *Texas Observer, ArtSpace, Mother Earth, Breathing the Same Air,* an East Tennessee anthology and other publications. She has won several awards for her short stories.

PATSY WARD BURK (Houston): The native Texan is one of the founders and a past President of the Woodlands Writers' Guild. She is a lecturer and author of short stories, poetry, and several novels. She has been published in *Touchstone, A View From the Edge, Housewife-Writers Forum*, the three *Suddenly* series, and several anthologies. Two of her myster/suspense novels, *The Knife Struck Four* and *Face of Betrayal*, are out in paperback. She is currently at work on another mystery novel.

BILLIE LOU CANTWELL (Trinity): Among others, she has published in TCU's *Descant, Waterways, Borderlands, Rosebud, California Quarterly, Capper's Weekly, Byline, Writer's Journal, The Writer* and *Papier Mache's* "When I'm An Old Woman, I Shall Wear Purple."

KRISTI CASSIN (Houston): She is an almost native Houstonian with midwestern roots, retired, widowed, with grown children scattered. She travels, writes and dabbles in photography. Previously published works are included in *Suddenly II* and *Suddenly III*.

JUNE SHORT CHALON (Bellaire): A native Houstonian, June has lived in rural Texas, France and Bolivia. She has been published by *Shelby County Historical Society,* the *Poetry Society of Texas* yearbooks and is the President of their Houston Chapter. She was recently appointed a Councilor for the organization.

BETH LYNN CLEGG (Houston): She is a fourth generation Texan who grew up in Austin. Her work has appeared in the *Houston Chronicle, Suddenly III, Texas Alcalde* and *Texas Poetry Calendar 2001*. Two anthologies, *Women Forged in Fire* and *Charity* are forthcoming in 2001.

JACK CRUMPLER (Willis): Jack is semi-retired from a career in journalism, public relations, advertising and marketing. He now works as a freelance writer, and has had four short stories published. His first novel is scheduled for publication this fall.

CAROLYN A. DAHL (Houston): She was an award winner in the 2000 Texas PEN Literary Contest, a 1997 and 1998 Juried Poet at the Houston Poetry Festival, and selected by Edward Albee for his playwriting workshop at the University of Houston. She is the author of "Transforming Fabric" (American Quilters' Society Press) and is working on a second art book for Watson-Guptill Publications (NY).

CHERYL L. DANIEL (Sugar Land): She has been published in the *Houston Chronicle's Texas Magazine, Fort Bend Lifestyles,* and *Cowboy Sports and Entertainment.* Among other newsletters, she has written a regular column for the Houston Writers League's *Houston Writer.* Her first novel *Catch a Falling Star* is published by Hard Shell Word Factory, an electronic book and trade paperback.

RHEA DANIEL (Houston): Rhea works in the Registrar's Office at Rice University and is a former newspaper journalist.

ROYCE DAVIDSON (Plano): He is a December 2000 graduate of The University of Texas at Dallas with a degree in Literature. A friend once told him you have to live before you can write. He hopes the "house" he lives in fuctions well enough to do that.

BETTY DAVIS (Houston): She is a freelance writer and editor, and has called Houston home since 1947. Her work has appeared in many journals and anthologies and is currently in *New Texas* as well as two Internet publications.

ANDRE DE KORVIN (Houston): Born in Berlin, Germany of Russian parents, he was raised in Paris, France, came to the U.S. in 1960 and graduated with a Ph.D. in Mathematics from UCLA. He teaches Computer and Mathematical Sciences at the U. of Houston-Downtown. His first book of poems *The Four Hard Edges of War* came out in 1992 and was translated into Italian and published in a bilingual edition by Edizioni Cadmo (Florence, Italy 1999). He has been the featured and guest poet at the Houston Poetry Fest, and has been published in many literary magazines. He recently completed three manuscripts: "A One Winged Angel", "Dreaming Indigo Time" and "The Day Clocks Spoke Russian."

PAULINE M. DELANEY (Houston): Pauline is an almost native Houstonian who has been "hooked" on stories all her life. She told them before she knew which end of a pencil to use and has written them ever since.

WENDY DIMMETTE (Dallas): She earned a M.A. from SMU with a creative thesis in poetry. Her poetry has appeared in *Espejo, Re: Artes*

Liberales, Poetry Society of Texas Year Books, Square Magazine, National Federation of State Poetry Societies, A Galaxy of Verse, and other publications. Five children's plays have been performed at Cabbages and Kings Theatre for Children, and she has conducted poetry workshops at Eastfield College.

JAMES O. DOBBS (Marshall): He is a native Texan, a member of the Rusk County Poetry Society, Poetry Society of Texas, Missouri State Poetry Society, and American Mensa. He is a watercolorist and retired minister.

YOLANDA FALCON (Houston): She earned a Bachelor's Degree in Psychology from the University of Houston, has taught calligraphy and other arts and crafts workshops and considers herself a "writer under construction." Recently her essay appeared in the *Houston Chronicle's* "Simple Sustenance Food Section." She writes short plays and monologues.

JOYCE M. FISCHER (Houston): Her fiction and poetry have appeared in *Suddenly III, The Snake Nation Review, The Ledge, Whiskey Island, Ark* and *The Connecticut Writer*. She has also written a novel called "The Donut Shop." Her nonfiction has appeared in *The New York Times, Family Life, Private Clubs* and *HOW* magazine.

LOUISE GAYLORD (Houston): She has co-authored three books on party planning in Houston: *Catering in Houston, Places to Take a Crowd in Houston,* and *Catering to Houston*. She edited and contributed to *Opera Cues* the Houston Grand Opera Guild magazine, and has received both short story and long fiction awards. Backdoor Theatre in Wichita Falls produced her full-length play *The Season*. Her work has also appeared in *Suddenly 98, Suddenly II* and *Suddenly III*.

KAREN GERHARDT (Weslaco): Karen is a former Houstonian who now lives and works in the Lower Rio Grande Valley.

J. LEE GOODMAN (Wichita Falls): She has been writing poetry since 1977 and is a member of the Wichita Falls Poetry Society of Texas. She works for the Wichita Falls ISD in the Science Resource Center and volunteers as tour guide and curriculum writer for the local nature center.

JOHN GORMAN (Galveston): He has taught literature and creative writing at the University of Houston-Clear Lake since its founding in 1974. Two of his chapbooks, *Perry Como Sings* and *Public Places*, were published by Mac*Kinations Press. A third, *The Oxford of the Floodplain*, was printed by UH-CL as part of its 20th Anniversary celebration. With recent work in *Suddenly III, Blue Violin, Curbside Review* and the *Houston Poetry Fest Anthology,* he received a second place in the Valentine's Day Love Poetry Slam at Mausoleum in Houston's historically marginal Montrose District.

NANCY GUSTAFSON (Huntsville): She is a wife, mother and grandmother who loves to write, read, sew, garden and cook. She has published poetry in several anthologies and poetry journals.

ALBERT HALEY (Abilene): He is writer in residence at Abilene Christian University. He is the author of *Home Ground: Stories of Two Families and the Land* and the novel *Exotic*. His fiction has also appeared in *Suddenly II, New Texas 2000, Christianity and the Arts, and The Mars Hill Review.*

JOYCE POUNDS HARDY (Houston): Joyce is a native Houstonian, a graduate of Rice University, mother of five, grandmother of thirteen, winner of The Texas Writer's Recognition Award presented by the Texas Institute of Letters in 1989, and publisher of two books of poetry.

JOYCE HARLOW (The Woodlands): She grew up in Sunfish, Kentucky on a farm with eight brothers and sisters, but has lived in Texas for over twenty years. She holds a B.A. and M.Ed. in Education and is the owner of Summerfield Academy in Spring. Her short fiction "The Stranger" was published in *Suddenly 98*, "Ashes" in *Suddenly II* and "Mad Dog" in *Suddenly III*.

LINDA J. HELMAN (The Woodlands): She is Treasurer of the Woodlands Writers' Guild, has been published in *Suddenly* and placed in a number of contests. A full-time tax accountant and owner of an Internet gift shop at www.4specialtygifts.com, she is currently working on a fiction novel.

DOROTHY HERRON (Houston): She currently teaches pre-school children with disabilities in HISD. She was adjunct professor at both Houston Community College and University of Houston Downtown teaching English as a Second Language. In the distant past she was a newspaper journalist.

BRADLEY EARLE HOGE (Spring): He is an at-home Dad for two little boys. He earned a Ph.D. in Paleoecology and a Masters in Education. He serves as "Dr. Brad the Science Dad" for his sons' preschool. Among others, his poetry has appeared in *Borderlands, Texas Poetry Review, Rattle, Minimus, The Dead Mule, fractal,* and *Everywhere is Someplace Else* from Plain View Press. Another poem is forthcoming from this press and his work appears in *Singularities* out in May. He was selected as a juried poet for the 2000 Houston Poetry Fest.

JAMES HOGGARD (Wichita Falls): He is the McMurtry Distinguished Professor of English at Midwestern State University in Wichita Falls, and was named the Texas State Poet Laureate for 2000. A former NEA Fellow and past president of The Texas Institute of Letters, he has authored numerous literary works throughout his career, including essays, short stories, plays and hundreds of poems. Of his fifteen books published, his poetry book *Medea in Taos* (Pecan Grove Press) was nominated for the Violet Crown Award, and *Rain in a Sunlit Sky* (Page One Publications) came out in 2000.

J. PAUL HOLCOMB (Double Oak): He is the President of the Poetry Society of Texas. He has authored one chapbook of poems, co-authored a children's book, and has over one hundred poems in various literary journals and anthologies. He is a retired software engineer.

GUIDA JACKSON (The Woodlands): In 2000, her fiction appeared in *Texas Short Stories II, Suddenly III*, and *New Texas 2000*. She has published 18 books and two CD-ROMs, one out in 2001 by Heritage Books. As Panther Creek Press, she publishes other people's fiction and poetry.

GRETCHEN LONG JAMESON (Houston): She received a BA in Literature from the University of Colorado, but has lived in Houston many years. She is wife, mother, volunteer, and new writer.

RAMONA JOHNS (Houston): She is an attorney and former Houston judge who now writes freelance. Her first book was *Children and the Law in Texas, What Parents Should Know* from University of Texas Press, 1999.

LISA KAHN (Houston): She was born in Berlin, received a B.S. from the U. Of Washington, and a PhD from the University of Heidelberg in Germany. She taught in Houston for many years, last at TSU, and published three anthologies, three prose volumes and twelve books of poetry in Germany, the U.S. and Switzerland. She has received many awards and was named Poeta Laureata at the U. of New Mexico in 1996.

JEANA KENDRICK (Conroe): She is managing editor for the *Door of Hope Magazine* as well as Communications Director overseeing the quality and on-time production of Door of Hope International's USA and Canadian publishing concerns. Her work has appeared in various newspapers and books, recently in *Fall From Innocence* (Page One Publications), *Suddenly* and *Suddenly II* (Martin House). Her first novel *Traffic* will be out soon. "The Last Bridge Across Mostar" is near completion and "Memoirs of a Bible Smuggler" is in the working stage.

KIMBERLY KING (Richardson): Her work has appeared in *Sojourn, Visions in Ink,* and *Southern Register*. She won second place in the Texas Association of Creative Writing Teachers 2000 and another story won first place in the Gulf Coast Association of Creative Writing Teachers 2000 and was read in the 2000 Dallas Museum of Arts reading series "Arts and Letters Live." She also read at "Faulkner on the Fringe 2000."

MAXINE B. KOHANSKI (Houston): Born in Eastern Canada, she has won numerous writing awards, been published in anthologies, newspapers and greeting cards in the U.S. and Canada. In 1991 she published her first book of poetry titled *Going Home*. In 1998 she received the Poetry Guild's grand prize. In 1999 she received a national honorable mention for a collection of her poems and was published in six national publications. She is currently the president of Poets Northwest in Houston.

KAREN O. KRAKOWER (Houston): A Houstonian for forty years, with a twenty year career in academic/medical publications and books. She has freelanced as a humorist in script, video, and speeches. Her play "Cat Tales" has been produced and her work has appeared several times in the *Houston Chronicle*.

WILLIAM H. LAUFER (The Woodlands): A visual artist by vocation, his translations of selected portions of the Sanskrit RG VEDA and BHAGAVAD GITA appeared in 1999 and 2000.

VANESSA LEVRIER LEGGETT (Houston): Vanessa lectures in English and criminology and is a writer in the true-crime genre. She has had scholarly works published, but considers her short story in *Suddenly* the first small step toward a career in crime fiction.

IRENE LESLIE (Bellaire): She was born in London, but has lived in the Houston area for the past forty-seven years. She is retired from selling residential real estate and finds great satisfaction in creative writing.

PEGGY ZULEIKA LYNCH (Austin): She is a native Texan, Poet Laureate, Poet-in-Residence at the Paris American Academy and Founder of Poetry in the Arts, Austin's longest running poetry venue.

JEANETTE McSHERRY (Spring): She is a past contributor to *Suddenly* and a member of The Woodlands Writers Guild, She has won awards for poetry, short story, childrens' and young adult fiction. In 2000 she won awards for both her fantasy novel *Touch of the North Star* and *Fire*, an adult contemporary fiction.

LIANNE ELIZABETH MERCER (Fredericksburg): Her work has appeared recently in *New Texas 2000* and *Suddenly III*. A Certified Poetry Therapist, she works with individuals and groups interested in the healing poem-making process.

BETH MILES (Huntsville): She is a native Texan who retired in 1998 from Sam Houston State University where she was Assistant Director for University Advancement.

REECE NEWTON (Cleona, Pa): He grew up in Beaumont, graduated from Lamar, taught college English and studied in Arizona and Illinois. He lived and taught in Guatemala and Spain, now lives in Pennsylvania and writes in his spare time. He was published in *Suddenly III*.

VIOLETTE NEWTON (Beaumont): Violette is a member of the Southeast Texas Womens Hall of Fame, and is a much published and much honored Poet Laureate of Texas.

MICHAEL POEHLS (Houston): He is a native Texan. He says his roots are entwined with those of the cedars and pines of East Texas, and his lungs are filled with the petro-chemical incense of East Houston.

SHIRLEY COUVILLION-POWELL (Houston): Shirley is a member of the Poetry Society of Texas and National Federation of State Poetry Societies. She has published in poetry anthologies at local, state and national levels, including *Lucidity,* and her poetry has been read on PBS television's "Freedom to Read." She has proofed and edited for a small newspaper, a newsletter and does freelance prose.

KATHLEEN R. RAPHAEL (El Paso): She is a freelance writer and college writing instructor. She writes fiction, non-fiction and poetry. Her work has appeared in regional and national publications, including *Suddenly II.*

CAROL J. RHODES (Houston): Her work, including poetry and fiction, has appeared in *Suddenly I, Suddenly II* and *Suddenly III*. She is also widely published in newspapers, journals, anthologies and business publications, and was recently runner-up in *Amelia Island's* fourth annual poetry and short story contest for her story "The Power of Prayer."

JAMES MICHAEL ROBBINS (Austin): He is the editor of *Sulphur River Literary Review*. His poetry has appeared in *Black Moon, The Bitter Oleander, Borderlands, Concho River Review, CutBank, Heeltap, Lynx Eye, Rattle*, and others. A chapbook, *Graviture*, has just been released by Rancho Loco Press.

CHRIS ROGERS (Hilltop Lakes): She has been published in novel-length suspense fiction, short story and has had a short play produced. *Chill Factor*, the third in the Dixie Flannigan series, came out in February 2000 in hard cover and in March 2001 in paperback.

CLAIRE OTTENSTEIN-ROSS (Pinehurst) is an award winning poet and author of eleven books. She has published in *Touchstone, Who's Who in Texas Letters*, and in magazines and anthologies in secular and inspirational areas. The retired President/Editor of Counterpoint Publishing Co., she co-founded Poets Northwest, Houston Northwest Inspirational Writers Alive! and Christian Writers Northwest. The 1998 Poetry Society of Texas Book of the Year was dedicated to her for promoting poetry in Texas.

JANE BUTKIN ROTH (Bellaire): Her poetry has recently appeared or is forthcoming in the *Austin Writer,* the *Windsor Review: A Journal of the Arts, Essential Love, Mothers and Daughters* and *Haiku-Sine,* an anthology of food-related haiku by Texans.

JANET HULL RUFFIN (Houston): Janet is an artist, writer and educator. She was part of the team that created the Rehabilitative Arts Project for Harris County Juvenile Probation and is currently full-time artist/facilitator for MD Anderson Cancer Hospital in Pediatrics.

ANNETTE SCHWARTZ (Houston): Annette is a swimmer, bowler, dancer, grandmother, and has won prizes for poetry in local, state and national contests. Her poems have appeared in several anthologies.

NAOMI STROUD SIMMONS (Fort Worth): She is active in local poetry groups, sponsors an eighth grade poetry club and assists with poetry in a high school creative writing class. She is an officer in the Poetry Society of Texas, has authored six books of poetry with poems published in *Galaxy, Lucidity, Grassland, National Federation of State Poetry Societies* and the *Poetry Society of Texas* year books, plus numerous anthologies.

KATHERINE SORRELL (Houston): She is a Junior at Kinkaid School who enjoys swimming and traveling.

LORI ANN STEPHENS (Richardson): She is a Ph.D. student at The University of Texas at Dallas. She recently edited three editions of *Sojourn,* the interdisciplinary arts journal at UTD, and is now working on her second novel.

CHUCK TAYLOR (College Station): Chuck is the author of two collections of short stories, *Lights of the City* and *Somebody to Love*. He has operated *Slough Press* since 1973 and teaches at Texas A&M.

CAROL KINCHELOE TESCH (Houston): A native Texan writer and painter, she has lived in Egypt, Malta, Saudi Arabia and Malaysia. She presently teaches art in the Continuing Education Department of Houston Community College and is an artist associate for the Art League of Houston.

JACK L. THOMAS (Houston): He has published *Whirling Fire*, an illustrated book of poetry based on his military experiences in Vietnam, written a Vietnam War memoir, a collection of motorcycling essays and is currently shaping his first novel which was a finalist in the mystery/suspense category of the 2001 Houston Writers Conference. An essay about miscreant youths in '50's suburban Houston appeared in the *Houston Tribune*.

MARK THONSSEN (Friendswood): He has lived in Texas for twenty years and works as an electrical engineer on Space Station simulators at the NASA Johnson Space Center. He writes as a hobby, having studied creative writing with B.K. Reeves. This is his first published story.

CAROLYN TOURNEY (Houston): She is a writer, visual artist and garden designer. Her degrees are in Geology and Fine Arts (painting). Her poetry has been published in the Texas anthology *Suddenly III*. She is presently working on collections of her poetry and short fiction.

MARK TWEEDY (Plano): Mark is a screenwriter, technology consultant and graduate of The University of Texas, Austin. He now lives in Berlin, Germany.

BEV VINCENT (The Woodlands): He is President of the Woodlands Writers' Guild and has written over sixty book reviews for the *Conroe Courier*. He also writes a bimonthly column for *Cemetery Dance* magazine.

SUE PETERS VOLK (Houston): She grew up in Denver, and earned a degree in music at Wichita State University in Kansas. She and her husband have lived in San Francisco, Houston and Melbourne, Australia, but returned to Houston in 1991. She attends continuing education classes at Rice University.

LEONA WELCH (Denison): She promotes poetry by participation. She serves the Poetry Society of Texas as Corresponding Secretary, Councilor, and Chairs the program of Poetry in Schools.

GERALD R. WHEELER (Katy): His photography, fiction and prose have appeared in *Pivot, Potomac Review, The MacGuffin, (JAMA), The Writer RE:AL, Kaleidoscope, Chiron Review* and elsewhere. His poetry collection, *Tracers* (Black Bear Publications) is out and his poetry collection "Tracks" (Timberline Press) will be out in 2002. He was nominated for the 2000 Western Writers of America Spur Award in Poetry.

LOUNELL WHITAKER (Beaumont): She is a member of the Beaumont Chapter of the Poetry Society of Texas. She has been published in the *Poetry Society of Texas* Year Books, *Suddenly, RSPC* Year Books and has written a chapbook *Apples From My Orchard.*

CYNTHIA WIER (Houston): She is a former advertising copywriter who has been writing poetry, short fiction and essays for ten years. A recent empty-nester, she enjoys family history, jaunts to antique shops and museums, and travel.

BETTY WIESEPAPE (Richardson): She is a native Texan and teaches creative writing at The University of Texas at Dallas and Northlake College. Her fiction has appeared in a number of journals including *Blue Mesa Review, New Texas, Texas Short Fiction, Riversedge* and *Concho River Review.*

Colophon

Suddenly IV, consisting of 212 pages, was edited and typeset by Jackie Pelham on a Power Macintosh G3 using Times and Zap Chancery fonts; Patsy Burk did the final proofing; cover photo was selected by Jackie Pelham and the cover was designed by Jesse Johnson; the book was printed and perfect bound by Morgan Printing, Austin, Texas.

Suddenly is an independently published anthology with the purpose of showcasing the talent of Texas authors. No monetary rewards are received from individuals or organizations other than through sale of yearly publications.

Order copies of

Suddenly 98 - ISBN 0-9627844-2-7
Suddenly II - ISBN 0-9627844-3-5
Suddenly III - ISBN 0-9627844-4-3
Suddenly IV - ISBN 0-9627844-7-8

from
Stone River Press
2003 Corral Drive
Houston, TX 77090
281-440-6701
japelh@swbell.net

Suddenly IV is $10.00 plus applicable tax and $1.75 shipping—add 50 cents shipping for each additional book. Back issues of Suddenly are $6.00 each with tax and shipping as above.